"In taking the wealth of conceptual insight and
The Intelligent Organisation and applying it to t
nance, Beckford takes on a formidable task.
thought-provoking synthesis of ideas spanning systems thinking, ...
and political science which is interwoven with illustrative vignettes drawn from
a wide range of practical spheres."

—Dr Andrew Chilvers, Honorary Lecturer, Dept of Science, Technology,
Engineering and Public Policy (STEaPP),
University College London

"The events of 2020 and the uneven response of national states to the crises
once again confirm that whatever form governance may take, it needs to be
intelligent. Beckford makes an excellent case for treating any organization as a
system within a dynamic environment. This book should be read by every local
and national leader and its lessons should be applied broadly."

—Professor Miguel Angel Centeno, Musgrave Professor of Sociology,
Vice-Dean, Princeton School of International and Public Affairs,
Princeton University

"How we relate to and think about being governed has been turned on its head
by Covid-19. *The Intelligent Nation* provides a very timely and relevant reflection on the role of government and its power to intervene in our basic freedoms. John Beckford challenges our centralised and controlled state in a time
of crisis. *The Intelligent Nation* lays the keystone for a radical rethink on how we
are governed and makes a good case for decentralising power. Excellent!"

—Gill Morris, FCIPR, Chief Executive,
DevoConnect

"Warm, easy and yet very precise, this is a much-needed reflection on what a state
can do, and how it can do it better. Recent crises like Covid-19, as well as ongoing crises, such as climate change or the long recovery from 2008, have shown up
starkly how ill adapted states are to challenges of such complexity, or pervasive-
ness, or duration. This may be particularly so where the crises evolve slowly over
time, rather than emerge suddenly. The failure of states to respond positively to
the possibilities of the digital revolution has also been stark. Above all this is a
coherent way of exploring how we can organise states better, making them more
adaptive to the challenges of today, and more coherent in a digital age."

—Ronan Palmer, Director, Clean Economy, E3G

"*The Intelligent Nation* presents a provocative case for change, blending cybernetic insight with freedom by design. John Beckford incisively exposes the dysfunctional essence of modern state bureaucracies; 'Transformation must not be stifled by self-preserving, self-interested, cautious, creeping incrementalism'. Building intelligent services around citizens is our collective challenge."

—Richard Berry, Assistant Chief Constable,
Gloucestershire Police

"In this book, John Beckford has advanced the ideas articulated in his earlier seminal work on *The Intelligent Organisation* to a new level to advocate for The Intelligent Nation. With a bold sub-title of How to Organise a Country John draws on his cybernetic approach to analyse how in a post-Brexit and post-Covid-19 world, current governance forms and bodies are failing to manage the balance between freedom and control in such a way as to deliver the desired outcomes for citizens. With a more overtly political stance (in keeping with the shift in focus) than was evident in *The Intelligent Organisation* the argument highlights the need for Western governments to become more adaptive if they are not to lose their democratic legitimacy. In turn, citizens have a role to play in becoming more democratically engaged. The book is written in a persuasive and very readable style, with plenty of insightful illustrative case study vignettes. It should be required reading for anyone with responsibility for public services and infrastructure as well as more generally those with an interest in performance management."

—Professor Louise Cooke, School of Business and Economics,
Loughborough University

THE INTELLIGENT NATION

The Intelligent Nation proposes a systemic and radical transformation of the organisation, management, ownership and performance of the services of the state by capitalising on the potential offered by contemporary information capability and fulfilling the rights and obligations both to and of citizens.

In this book, John Beckford shows how, by adopting the principles of an Intelligent Organisation, the state can thrive and meet the needs of its citizens. He proposes a complete rethink of the state as the enabler or provider of public services. In particular, he points to the failure of the public sector to significantly emulate the massive gains in productivity and customer focus experienced in both manufacturing and services (e.g. finance, retailing, insurance). Governance and all public services must be redesigned to align to the contemporary needs of the citizen and exploit the power of information to enable a transformation of their effectiveness, redefine efficiency and support human-based services in crucial areas. Each chapter provides the key learning points, a discussion of the problem in theory and practice, integrated case studies and discussion points.

Written in an accessible style, the book provides thought-provoking supplemental reading for masters and undergraduate students reading organisation theory, organisation development, political science, public administration, healthcare, information systems and business and management science.

John Beckford is a partner in Beckford Consulting, Non-Executive Chair of the Board of Rise Mutual CIC, a Non-Executive Director of Fusion21 (a social enterprise) and CoreHaus and Visiting Professor in both the Department of Civil, Environmental and Geomatic Engineering at University College London and the Centre for Information Management, School of Business and Economics, Loughborough University.

Citizenship and Sustainability in Organizations
Series Editors: David F Murphy and Alison Marshall

Exploring how organizations and citizens respond to and influence current and future global transformations, this book series publishes excellent, innovative and critical scholarship in the fields of citizenship, social responsibility, sustainability, innovation, and place leadership in diverse organizational contexts. These contexts include commercial businesses, social enterprises, public service organizations, international organizations, faith-based organizations (FBOs), non-governmental organizations (NGOs), community groups, hybrids and cross-sector partnerships. The role of the individual as citizen may also be explored in relation to one or more of these contexts, as could formal or informal networks, clusters and organizational ecosystems.

The Intelligent Nation
How to Organise a Country
John Beckford

THE INTELLIGENT NATION

How to Organise a Country

John Beckford

Routledge
Taylor & Francis Group

LONDON AND NEW YORK

First published 2021
by Routledge
2 Park Square, Milton Park, Abingdon, Oxon OX14 4RN

and by Routledge
52 Vanderbilt Avenue, New York, NY 10017

Routledge is an imprint of the Taylor & Francis Group, an informa business

British Library Cataloguing-in-Publication Data
A catalogue record for this book is available from the British Library

Library of Congress Cataloging-in-Publication Data
Names: Beckford, John, 1958- author.
Title: The intelligent nation : how to organise a country / John Beckford.
Description: Abingdon, Oxon ; New York, NY : Routledge, 2021. | Series:
Citizenship and sustainability in organizations | Includes
bibliographical references and index. | Identifiers: LCCN 2020034698 | ISBN
9780367430559 (hbk) | ISBN
9780367430573 (pbk) | ISBN 9781003000990 (ebk)
Subjects: LCSH: Public interest. | Knowledge economy. | State, The. |
Organizational change. | Organizational effectiveness.
Classification: LCC JC330.15 .B44 2021 | DDC 320.1--dc23
LC record available at https://lccn.loc.gov/2020034698

ISBN: 978-0-367-43055-9 (hbk)
ISBN: 978-0-367-43057-3 (pbk)
ISBN: 978-1-003-00099-0 (ebk)

Typeset in Bembo
by SPi Global, India

CONTENTS

CASE STUDIES

FIGURES

TABLES

PREFACE

The conundrum to be addressed by any government at any time is to blend the liberty necessary for human freedom with those constraints essential to societal order, peace and tranquillity. Liberty stimulates capacity for aspiration and innovation to thrive enabling social and economic growth while constraints act to support equality of opportunity, social justice, economic fairness and defence of the realm. Achieving this blend relies on resolving the tension between laissez-faire and interventionism by posing them as complementary rather than alternate. Rather than preferring either, The Intelligent Nation must achieve both appropriately to its complex needs.

The argument of this book is that the current organisation and systems of governance and, in some cases, the government itself, are unfit for the contemporary challenges faced by states. While the organisation of most countries has evolved in a piecemeal manner, the essential orientation of most states is traditional, functional and bureaucratic. The philosophy of national organisation and its form are especially crucial at a time when emergent technologies and availability of data can enable surveillance and intervention on a scale never seen before. As this book is being completed, the exit of the United Kingdom from the European Union and the emergence of the Covid-19 global pandemic are generating challenges to government and electors alike in a manner not experienced for more than 40 years. Potential interventions are not limited to domestic government but extend to commercial providers of technology and, as always, governments of other nations. The freedom and liberty of citizens increasingly depend on discipline by government, the discipline NOT to intervene and NOT to permit intervention by either state or private actors. It is a philosophical and moral requirement rather than a technical or economic argument that just because the government can intervene it does not mean it should. While many interventions may be defended as protective or preventative, such interventions must pass a test of reasonableness. As Spencer[1] put it 'the ultimate result of protecting men from the results of their folly is to end with a nation of fools' and, in the UK, while many perceive that the so-called nanny state is intervening where it would be better not, others are calling for further intervention in the wake of 'austerity' and the Covid-19 pandemic. Failure to resolve the tension between freedom and control risks anarchic or totalitarian outcomes. The tension must be resolved yet the currently adopted, functionally arranged and centralised activities and processes of government and governance cannot achieve it. A new model is required which, while continuing to allow for the fallibility of its human actors, seeks to optimise the balance of freedom and constraint, of liberty and control, of stability and adaptation – The Intelligent Nation.

Achieving an Intelligent Nation requires us to challenge and completely rethink the state as the enabler or provider of public services; it demands that national governance and public services continually, radically and discontinuously evolve to meet the always changing needs of the citizens. This rethinking must exploit the power of information realised through the application of contemporary technologies to enable a transformation in effectiveness and the redefinition of the efficiency of national governance and state administration.

Thinking systemically, we must consider the whole state, its constituent parts and its international relationships as the context in which it adds value to the nation by protecting and promoting itself. The trick to be achieved is to ensure that public services meet the requirements of all at a supportable social, economic and environmental cost. The thinking, based on the ideas of Intelligent Organisation (Beckford, 2020), shows that effective support to enable the resilience of each individual citizen will reduce the extent to which they are reliant upon the state. Freedom from intervention for those equipped to cope for themselves and meaningful and valuable support for those who require it follows, reducing demand for state provision. Asserting the power of decision of the individual and decentralising state power from national to regional and local authorities allows the individual citizen to thrive while operating within a coherent social context that balances the individual interest with that of wider society.

This book explores the current state of affairs before considering how a new model of a resilient and sustainable country emerges from the synthesis of nation and state. Rooted in the organisationally cybernetic model of The Intelligent Organisation, this offers an alternative set of arrangements rooted in democracy, systemic understanding and distributed power. The sustainability and resilience of the individual citizen are then considered before an examination of how the social infrastructure of public services can be reorganised to support citizens better. The systemic relationships of the fundamental infrastructure on which the whole country depends is then reviewed before, and finally, a new model for understanding the performance of the country is developed.

An Intelligent Nation requires governance and organisational arrangements which are focused on citizen outcomes and capable of continual adaptation to changing circumstances. An Intelligent Nation balances the economic imperative to generate more value than it consumes, with the social imperative to support and enable each citizen to the extent that they need it and the environmental imperative to minimise the harm done. Given the complexity of contemporary societies, some citizens will always need support to cope while all citizens will sometimes need it. An approach rooted in the idea of The Intelligent Nation resolves the tension between maximising individual autonomy and maintaining coherence. It nurtures the sense of shared identity and from this arises significant challenges to ensure democratic consent and the legitimacy of the state: government, law, regulation and provision of state services to the public.

The book is finished, the arguments are just starting.

Note

1. http://thisiscommonsense.com/2019/07/07/herbert-spencer-4-2-2/ 30/12/2019

ACKNOWLEDGMENTS

Any book such as this benefits from the work of many other than the named author. First among those are the many writers whose work has been drawn upon in developing the ideas and argument, I have noted those contributions in the usual way. Second are the numerous people over several years and with widely differing views with whom some or all of these arguments and ideas have been explored. Those debates have informed and developed my thinking. Third in this case are a group of people who have contributed case studies or vignettes to assist in illustrating the points made, their contributions are invaluable. I am grateful to:

Professor Brian Collins, Founding Convenor, UKCRIC

Rev. Keith Elford, Director, Elford Consulting

An immigrant who wishes to remain anonymous

Dr. Boulent Imam, University of Surrey

Chris Murray, Executive Director, Core Cities Group

Mr. Chris Singer, NPCC (Rtd), Resilience Advisers

Professor Peter Kawalek, Loughborough University

Dr. Donya Hajializadeh, University of Surrey

Dr. Tom Dolan, Senior Research Associate, UKCRIC

Dr. Charles House, Medical Director, University College London Hospitals

A small group of reviewers have undertaken the substantial task of reading the manuscript during production and offered always helpful guidance, comments and suggestions. As always such contributions lead to improvement. The mistakes, errors and omissions are all mine.

Finally, my thanks to Sara, Paul, Matthew and Victoria who challenge and support me in equal measure.

1

THE DYSFUNCTIONAL STATE AND THE STATE OF THE PROBLEM

Introduction

The Intelligent Nation is a synthesis of the people, who constitute that nation, and the state, the system of government and governance through which it emerges. Our individual and shared histories inform our individual and shared identities; the problem for the state is that maintaining its relevance to those identities, and its efficiency and effectiveness, requires it to persistently reinvent its ways of being and doing. The citizen engagement through which government acquires democratic legitimacy must be reaffirmed while the delivery of social and physical infrastructure must reflect contemporary understanding of organisation, the power of technology and the right of the individual to self-determination. Transformation is required to overcome growing democratic deficits, to realise potential and to overcome centralising tendencies and functional, producer-led thinking.

The combined mechanisms of governance, civil and military public services and administration, collectively known as 'the state', are typically non-adaptive bureaucratic structures designed to solve problems we had and not the problems we have now; that they resist change is what once made them useful but now they obstruct. The bureaucrats and the bureaucratic system acknowledge the need to change, perhaps mimic the philosophy and language of the desired future then co-opt it within the existing paradigm; the potential for real change is smothered. Although there are incremental gains in reported productivity, the transformational potential of contemporary thinking about organisation, fully utilising the skills and abilities of people and the scope for contemporary information systems to enable radical reinvention of public services, is suppressed by the immune system of the bureaucracy.

The contemporary structure of 'the state' began to emerge in England in 1215 with the signing of the Manga Carta, though some would argue that the Domesday Book, commissioned in 1085, constituted the first modern register of national assets and the basis of a national system of taxation. Other states are much more recent with modern France emerging following the revolution in 1789, modern Germany in 1871 with its reunification in 1990, the Kingdom of Italy in 1861, the Commonwealth of Australia in 1901 and the USA in 1776. It is to these entities that the notion of 'nationality' belongs while there are a vast array of other sub-national identities arising from loyalties to regions or locations, to racial groups, clans and tribes.

States have evolved rather than been designed but their evolution has not kept pace with social and technological changes nor those in their natural, political or economic environments. Current arrangements will not suffice. State mechanisms intended to generate stability, integrity and coherence lag behind the evolution of society, their inertia acting to reinforce the status quo, inhibiting challenge and innovation. Confronted with the contemporary challenges of the Covid-19 pandemic, the compelling environmental case for decarbonisation, emerging threats to freedom from governmental and commercial use of digital technologies for surveillance and the continuing issues of poverty, hunger, exclusion, lack of education, healthcare and employment across much of the planet, established state organisations are stumped. Meanwhile a range of supranational organisations, both governmental and not, have arisen posing perhaps a greater risk to our freedoms. Unaccountable to the electorate of any country, they have powers of surveillance beyond those imaginable a few years ago.

This chapter considers these challenges through the lenses of the centralisation of power, functional organisation, the pursuit of effectiveness, the state of technology and the criticality of democracy before considering the potential for transformation.

Bureaucracy and the centralisation of power

Over many years, many centuries in some cases, states have accreted power and control, parts have been added, existing parts extended, conflicts avoided by the development (consciously or not) of duplicated and overlapping services. In evolutionary terms, while co-adaptation of the limbs of the state has generated new capabilities, those parts which are no longer effective have not necessarily been made redundant. The result, however unintended, is that citizens sometimes experience it as a sclerotic and pathologically auto-poietic system more focused on its own well-being than the fulfilment of its purpose. Friedman (1982) suggests 'the great threat to freedom is the concentration of power' while Sampson (1993) described how power had been centralising for many years in the UK, and Beer (1993) showed how the connectedness of social systems acts to sustain the existing order in any human system inhibiting both social and economic mobility. Beckford (1994) showed that capital, of all types, whether economic, social, political or informational, tends to centralise acting as a barrier to the distribution of power and influence potentially trapping people in their current relative position. The state, in most cases, is the largest and most powerful aggregator of capital for any country enjoying all-pervading influence in the economy and society through taxation, benefits, regulation and legislation and public spending. There is appeal for the state in pursuing the notional efficiency gains arising from better information and more centralised control but as will be shown, the loss of citizen freedom and autonomy outweighs the benefit. These characteristics are not solely products of human decisions but are inherent in the systemic structure of the complex dynamical but non-adaptive organisation which, because of the centralisation of power, reinforces the status quo. When centralisation of power acts to unduly restrict the freedom of the individual, then 'we would be certain to create a stagnant society with all the characteristic of unfreedom' (Hayek, 2006). Deliberate and disruptive human intervention in the operation of the system is required to overcome the centralising tendency inherent in the bureaucratic model.

Weber (1924) wrote of the 'technical superiority' of bureaucracy which has become the dominant form of organisation. He recognised a useful distinction between the exercise of power and that of authority: the former seen by Pugh & Hickson (1989) as being 'the ability to force people to obey' while the latter they interpret as where 'orders are voluntarily obeyed'. We will use 'voluntarily' to mean that the individual has a meaningful choice.

Weber went on to describe 'three pure types of legitimate authority': rational-legal, traditional and charismatic. He saw the legitimacy of the first, rational-legal authority, in 'acceptance of the right of those elevated to authority to issue commands'. The second, traditional authority, drew its legitimacy from custom and practice. The third, charismatic authority, drew on 'devotion to the specific and exceptional sanctity, heroism or exemplary character of an individual person'. Weber asserted an 'urgent need for stable, strict, intensive and calculable administration', asserting that bureaucracy must have 'a crucial role in our society' as the 'central element' in any kind of large-scale administration.

The critical aspects of rational-legal authority with a bureaucratic (in the non-pejorative sense) organisation are a reliance on obedience to the established consistent norms and rules, acceptance that authority is impersonal and belongs to the office rather than the office holder, with obedience expected from members to the 'law' not the individual. That all requires a rule-based organisation with defined competence (authority to decide as opposed to capability or skill), a hierarchical system of offices (the bureaux), technical and normative (values and beliefs based) rules and separation of the role of 'owner' from that of office holder. While many of our contemporary organisations are larger, more complex, more diverse and more global than anything that might have been envisaged by Weber, the relationships and interactions within and between them are also more far-reaching socially, economically and politically; nonetheless, many of them still reflect this definition. Inevitably, the traditional and charismatic authorities blend with the dominant 'rational-legal' form, and it is through them that the political dimension of organisational life is played out. What is experienced as 'office-politics' comes into play when individual leaders draw on traditional loyalty to a position or charismatic attraction to a personality to draw the loyalty of staff to themselves, rather than the office or the organisation.

Ultimately, all states, whatever their form of government, bring state services together in one overarching structure through their own single system of governance. The ultimate 'senior management' is the government, necessarily political, responsible for setting policy and strategy and both overseeing and supporting the various public services to which it is committed. The bureaucratic structure is necessarily centralising; it places power in the hands of a few and requires all others to follow their dictat, to conform to the bureaucracy.

All organisations, however bureaucratic, are also political; their human actors are informed by desires, hopes, beliefs and expectations. Whereas the state is explicitly political, in those entities we more normally think of as organisations (e.g., companies, partnerships, clubs, civil and military services of various types), the politics are implicit and subsumed in the hierarchies of ownership, managership or bureaucratic control. However, when we observe organisations, the politics make themselves evident in the behaviours of individuals, the exercise of power, the decisions that are made (or not), the people and things which are valued (or not). The politics become translated into the way the organisation is run: its bureaucracy.

For most states, the government is formed primarily from the members of political parties who are elected to the parliament. These parties are tribes or clans, founded on a shared set of beliefs and values, with aspirations to run the country in their own image. Their very existence acts as a filter on what it is possible to do but, more worryingly, because of party loyalties, can act to limit what it is acceptable for an individual to say. Loyalty to a party can overwhelm loyalty to an idea or a country. Each party enters an election with a manifesto, a set of intentions it will seek to fulfil if elected to office. The manifesto is a periodic codification of the expressed beliefs of the party and potentially has the effect of limiting what is politically and socially acceptable. Policy then emerges from the manifesto with alignment being key to the idea of belongingness for members; divergence from the party line is actively discouraged. The filter of 'party' on the values and ideas of the individual politician generates a circumstance where the party does not do what is wanted or needed but what is 'clubbable' or tolerable. Considered from that perspective, there is a whole new discussion to be held about the extent to which a political party should receive funding from the state or other large organisations. While such funding may allow a minority party to more rapidly grow and influence the whole, secure financing reinforces the position of the established parties and risks reducing their responsiveness to public opinion since their existence does not rely on financial support from individuals.

All decisions ultimately reflect the values and beliefs of the decision maker limited by the rules and constraints of the system in which they operate (to the extent that they are observed). The impact of decisions internal to an organisation and the underlying drivers are commonly related to the economic well-being of that organisation and the expectations of the owners or providers of capital; not necessarily the same thing.

Functional or systemic organisation

Commonly departments of the state, because of their processes, behaviours and supporting information systems, fail to realise the potential of either substantial developments in digital capability or the change in our understanding of human needs and behaviours. Consequently, they fail to emulate the gains in productivity achieved from applied information technology and customer focus in commercial organisations. Government, in the UK at least, has a poor record in procuring and implementing information systems-based change and continues to work with customer-inefficient systems. Breaking out from this would generate the potential for a step change in the productivity, efficiency and effectiveness of state provision and allow the capability of the human actors within those organisations to be realised; the state might thrive and meet the needs of its citizens.

Arranged functionally rather than around customer-focused processes, attention is paid to accountability for resources rather than achievement of desired outcomes. Continuation of that approach will not suffice for the future. Some parts don't work well while some parts perhaps don't work at all; the financial cost (met through various forms of taxation) and the social cost (met through service failure and time impositions on the lives of citizens) are both unsupportable. It seems that in many situations, the current approaches demand too much of the citizen and give too little benefit, failing in both regards to acknowledge and respond to the opportunities and potential available through contemporary management thinking and emerging technology. Is it not time for a wholesale redesign, a reinvention? The following example is not untypical, everybody is following the bureaucracy.

Unconscious profligacy: Dr. John Beckford

A small, volunteer run charity applied to a public sector body for a small but significant grant to be paid and accounted for annually over 4 years. The grant was duly approved but strangely for only 3 years instead of 4.

At the end of the first year the programme had under-recruited and failed to find suitable premises for one of its events. It therefore returned the unused portion of the grant (around one-third) and requested a reduced grant for the following year.

Rather than simply reducing the grant, the public authority instructed the charity, which had been totally compliant with its requests, to reapply for the smaller grant. It duly did so, requiring much additional work by the volunteers, and waited some time for a response. Meanwhile because of the arising financial uncertainty, some commitments could not be made, some opportunities to recruit were lost. Nonetheless, the grant ultimately came through, the work continued.

The small charity continued to report as requested, keeping the public authority fully aware of progress.

In year three, the grant did not arrive on time. It appeared that a change of personnel meant the payment was not made, because of the arising financial uncertainty some commitments could not be made, some opportunities to recruit were lost.

Towards the end of year three, it was realised that the funding agreement was terminating a year earlier than expected. The director of the small, volunteer run charity spoke to the executive of the public authority on this.

"Mmmm, that is not good, you will need to reapply but we don't have a form yet so resubmit the old one suitably modified."

The director of the small, volunteer run charity for the third time duly edited, revised and updated the form and submitted it to the Executive as requested.

Two days later, the director received an email from the commissioning officer at the public authority advising that the incorrect form had been used and the charity would need to resubmit with additional information on a revised form, a fourth go. (To be fair, the commissioning officer had transferred the bulk of the data to the new form).

Nobody is setting out to waste anybody's time and the defence of the Public Authority will be the need to demonstrate good custodianship of the public purse. However, the same grant will have been applied for three times, reviewed three times, approved three times when it should have happened once. The frustration for the small volunteer run charity is immense, distracting volunteer effort from the purpose to be fulfilled, creating unnecessary uncertainty, wasting public money.

A small example but one we can be sure is replicated many times across many public authorities, all of them unconsciously profligate because their QC, reengineered, lean and austere processes are focused on internal accountability not achievement of desired outcomes!

Nobody set out to design an inefficient system, nobody intended to cause the same work to be done three times; it is a consequence of the design of the organisation, its processes and the financial rules. The cost to the charity of complying with the processes is not taken into account when judging the efficiency of the bureaucracy which itself only measures the efficiency with which the process is carried out, not recognising the number of times it is done!

Suffering the same dysfunctionally self-serving organisational struggles for control, power, efficiency and effectiveness as corporate organisations but lacking the financial constraint of the need for profitability, the implications of state waywardness are potentially far more wasteful, more damaging to the economy and to citizens than the, often stumbling, competence of corporates. This is because states have a far wider reaching impact on us across the whole of our lives, from birth to death. A commercial organisation when losing money may increase prices, reduce costs (or both), be acquired or go out of business. A public sector organisation when unable to operate within budget may overspend or, more frequently, abolish or limit the availability of services leading ultimately either to increased taxation or failure to meet the needs of the public and sometimes both! In the case of the UK, we can consider the much reported 'black hole'[1] in defence spending for capital equipment (commitments made that cannot be met within budget), the queues and 'rationing' by the NHS[2] and the declared inability to investigate crime[3] by some police forces; situations which some might suggest could be deliberately engineered. Whichever way it goes, the resulting cry is always for 'more resources'.

Challenging this functional approach is an emerging understanding and adoption of the need to address the world from a systemic (Ackoff, 1981) perspective. Slow to progress as it attempts to overcome the inertia of the embedded reductionistic approach, a systemic understanding is essential to the comprehension of complex dynamical systems and, applied wisely, leads to better outcomes for citizens. Adopting a systemic approach is difficult; it generates challenges from the existing arrangements and is often not well understood. A systemic research initiative, UK Collaboratorium for Research in Infrastructure and Cities (UKCRIC), has emerged to engineer the future infrastructure of the UK. This requires that the research community adopts a systemic mindset. The following section shows the challenges and the achievement.

UKCRIC: Professor Brian Collins, CB, FREng

The UK Collaboratorium for Research in Infrastructure and Cities (UKCRIC)[4] is establishing world-leading laboratories, urban observatories and modelling and simulation capabilities to provide a basis for the transformation of UK abilities to make infrastructure and city systems far more sustainable, resilient, liveable, adaptable and smart. UKCRIC is the collective outcome of a wide multi-disciplinary range of research programmes to guide those intervening in the systems-of-systems of infrastructure and cities.

As Chief Scientific Adviser from 2006 to 2011 in the Departments of Business and Transport, I recognised that transport, energy and digital were very closely interconnected and interdependent while natural disasters occurring in the UK and elsewhere made it apparent that water was also a critical infrastructural component on which we depended. None of them were being governed or invested in in a way that was fit for the future. These observations and experiences resulted in the generation of a report with which I was involved from the Council for Science and Technology (CST) (2009) for the Prime Minister of the UK in which there were 7 recommendations (here abbreviated).

Recommendation 1

Government needs to appoint a lead body to deliver a clear and consistent vision for the future of the National Infrastructure (NI) in order to create certainty, address both short- and longer-term pressures and changes, and attract investment to the UK. Government needs to decide where the lead should be. We believe BIS, Treasury and Cabinet Office are all well placed to act as the focal point within Government, but working with an independent stakeholder group of business and other major players. The vision should look forward to 2050, clearly setting out the objectives and the rationale for decision-making.

The government established Infrastructure UK within the Treasury which identified what programmes and projects were already being considered across departments; the output became the National Infrastructure Plan. This was in essence a shopping list but there was no vision or strategy with factors suggested as being the responsibility of an oversight body not completely considered. In 2014, notwithstanding changes of government, the debate for an arms-length body had crystallised into a recommendation called the National Infrastructure Commission (NIC) established in 2016. It now provides a framework for assessment of strategic need while Infrastructure UK has been merged with the Major Projects Authority to become the Infrastructure and Projects Authority (IPA).

Recommendation 2

Government must address urgently the silo-based approach to NI, in particular to agree that the lead department, working closely with Cabinet Office and the independent stakeholder group, should take the overall policy lead in co-ordinating across Government and that the overall objectives should be to:

- develop mechanisms for achieving a more joined-up approach across Government in order to deliver the vision and prioritise the resilience and interconnectivity issues that need to be tackled
- improve knowledge-sharing across Government, its agencies, business and the regulators to enable better risk assessment and alignment of regulation with policy objectives, as well as delivering better analysis and ensuring innovative solutions are transferred between the different sectors of the infrastructure
- implement the provisions of the Planning Act as a matter of urgency

The various parts of the NI operate in silos, with significant fragmentation of responsibilities and accountabilities across Government, its agencies, the regulators, its operators and at a geographic scale. Silos at the level of the individual, as well as at the organisational and legislative levels, need to be cleared away.

Despite the existence of the NIC and IPA, there still appears to be no body which puts together possible or plausible solutions to address needs and turn them into implementable missions or portfolios of programs.

Recommendation 3

The lead department, working closely with Cabinet Office and the independent stakeholder group, should collaborate with senior business leaders and the regulators to scope out and deliver by 2010 a road map setting out the priority actions in the short term (5 years) and for the longer-term, that are needed to enhance or maintain the resilience of the NI, paying particular attention to:

- points of weakness, especially vulnerabilities at the interconnections and how best to build in the necessary safeguards and redundancy into the systems to mitigate weak points
- conflicts created by different strategic and legislative frameworks, and understanding the effects of sector-specific interventions on other components of the NI
- stimulating better understanding of the complexity and resilience of the national infrastructure, by commissioning research into scenario planning and modelling NI systems, from physical, economic and social perspectives
- human factors, so that individuals operating in one sector of the NI consider the effects of what they do on other sectors of the NI
- technology and skills needs (see recommendations 5 and 7)

There is a lack of understanding of the vulnerabilities, particularly where one sector of the NI is dependent on another. Such dependencies can lead to a misplaced level of reliance on other systems that could also have serious consequences, for example, Internet-enabled ICT networks which are used to control parts of the NI.

This holistic recommendation addresses the systemic issues of infrastructure in a developed country stressed by exogenous factors such as extreme weather events, demographic change and resource scarcity. Legislative requirements on climate change which may be encapsulated in carbon emissions or in zero carbon manufacturing further stresses the need to close the gap between the NIC and the IPA. This must not only deal with infrastructure needs and solutions but also have greater understanding of delivery of those infrastructure solutions on all the other aspects of a developed countries existence.

Recommendation 4

Government, working closely with the Regulators and the major business stakeholders, should ensure that the remits of regulators are fit for purpose and in particular whether they:

- provide incentives for modernisation and innovation
- deliver the necessary resilience and interconnectedness within and between the different sectors of the NI

- stimulate innovative solutions where appropriate
- are joined-up in terms of how they work across boundaries between their respective regimes, and at the interconnectivities between different sectors of the NI

We recognise that this work will need to be carried out at a strategic level and avoid creating unnecessary uncertainty. Regulation of national infrastructure is needed because market forces alone may not provide all of the essential features of the NI, for example, the appropriate level of security, resilience, interconnectivity and co-ordination between infrastructures, research and development investment and future-proofing.

The current regulatory framework has lasted well over 20 years and was designed for particular purposes, separately for the individual sectors within the NI.

In 2015 a regulators network was created in order to provide a forum for regulators to share their impact one upon another. Initially meeting infrequently and not very visible, unable to take a strategic view of the role of regulation on infrastructure services and systems; the rules of engagement for operators, for investors and strategic thinkers changed little. This has improved markedly since climate change legislation and financial austerity have caused deeper conversations to occur within and between regulators. The pace of change of the total regulatory environment has been slow. While predictability of regulatory frameworks over periods of 10 to 15 years is necessary for infrastructure provision investment there is a tension between this and the rate of change necessary to cope with exogenous factors demanding urgent attention.

Recommendation 5

Government departments, the Regulators, the Research Councils and bodies such as the Technology Strategy Board need to incentivise the infrastructure operators to connect better to the science and engineering base to develop innovative solutions using best technology. To do this, they should come together to address the following core questions:

- is procurement being used optimally, or indeed at all, to balance low risk/low cost solutions with the need to innovative?
- whether there should be more, or more effective, Innovation Platforms, Knowledge Transfer Networks and other types of collaborative R&D projects between infrastructure operators, academia and the other stakeholders?
- what technologies are available now and are they being exploited effectively within NI?

- what are the barriers to deployment, for example, the need for technology demonstration?
- what are the priority areas for underpinning R&D?
- how to encourage more cross-disciplinary research to clarify the interconnections and interdependencies of infrastructure components, including the human dimensions?
- what scenario planning is needed?
- what roles the professional bodies and learned societies might play?

This recommendation was essentially the foundation for the creation of UKCRIC. Although the solutions that were available from within a university sector were necessarily partial nevertheless the vision as laid out to the then Department for Business Innovation and Skills was more holistic and did address as many of the issues raised above as was feasible. It is though very likely that a new Institute will need to be created to provide a systemic solution for the delivery of infrastructure research and innovation at a system level and at the scale and pace needed to address the issues.

Recommendation 6

Government should put in place ongoing mechanisms for gathering social intelligence for example public engagement and dialogue for key issues on the national infrastructure. The general business community and the wider public need to understand the challenges that will be faced by NI over the next 30–50 years. It is essential that the long-term provision of national infrastructure be informed by a better understanding of users' needs and expectations. These needs must be factored into all stages of the design, development and operation of infrastructure as strategies and policies develop, regulations evolve and investments are made.

We believe that Government, infrastructure businesses and regulators should put in place mechanisms for public engagement and dialogue on key issues such as:

- the value placed on infrastructure whose provision entails significant investments and costs
- its significant carbon footprint
- future challenges and the role customers can play in helping to address them
- levels of investment in the UK NI
- how tolerant society is to risks resulting from infrastructure failures
- how to achieve the necessary skills sets by attracting people to key industries
- how Government can better act as an intelligent customer

Some research programmes that have been set up to attempt to find out perceptions of social need for infrastructure but this recommendation has hardly been addressed at all. It would seem, however, particularly in the context of ageing population and extreme events, that the time is now right for much more research to be carried out at the national and local level in order that much stronger evidence base is provided for investment and intervention as appropriate. The Observatories component of UKCRIC provides a starting point for meeting some aspects of this recommendation.

Recommendation 7

The Sector Skills Councils, working with business, BIS and professional bodies urgently need to address the short-term gaps in the skills market to deliver a 21st century NI, and provide clear forecasts of the skills for the longer-term, and how these can be met. The operators of NI need to identify their needs to ensure they attract, retain and develop the skills of their workforces.

A clear vision of the skills required to operate, maintain, develop and modernise the national infrastructure needs to be developed. The operators of the NI have the central role in driving this forward. Engineering skills across all the major engineering disciplines will be central to delivering a modernised NI, on a major scale not seen in the last 50 years.

The Sector Skills Councils and other bodies representing industry and professions, such as learned societies, professional associations, higher and further education institutes, need to continue working together to provide the Government with this essential information. The development of multidisciplinary skills sets to design, install, operate and maintain the NI will be essential.

Social science knowledge, research capability and skills will be required across a range of disciplines such as transport planning, operational research, demography, social statistics, anthropology, geography, sociology, social psychology will be essential at many stages of planning and implementing change in the NI. These include:

- researching, and gathering together the findings from existing research on the social dimensions of modernising the NI
- informing modelling and simulation on a more interconnected NI
- operational management of the NI systems in a way which takes the social dimensions fully into account
- managing public engagement

The language used in this recommendation reflects the era in which it was made and various mechanisms available at the time of this report are no longer available. There have been developments in skills availability in certain areas particularly construction and advanced manufacturing and in digital. However, the lack of a more holistic view of the skills that are needed reflects the difficulty of pulling together what is a very disparate industry. It is needed in order to provide the case for investment in more broad-based skills and professionalism such that infrastructure delivery cost is reduced and its fidelity vastly improved. This area is particularly urgent if we are to meet the legal obligations of climate change and net zero carbon, explicitly in housing and other urban infrastructure where the complexity of interrelated solutions has to be taken into account at the design, implementation and operational phases. Without such skills development all other aspects of infrastructure thinking will founder because what is implemented will not meet the needs of society and the country will suffer economically and socially as a result.

Commentary

It has taken a decade for most but not all of the recommendations in the CST report to be at least in the course of being met. Implementation was consigned to a fragmented and uncoordinated set of actors, with no overarching convening body ensuring coherence of action. For an Intelligent Nation attempting to create a framework for delivery of a large-scale transformation of a set of national assets the lesson to be learnt is that a convening body is required to cover all aspects of the need and how it is to be met. That body should continue to exist for a suitably long period of time. This is particularly so during the design procurement and delivery and into operation of the capability and including the programme of skills development and of social consultation. The situation as it is now is that the remaining parts of the governance of the infrastructure modernisation programme could very easily be put in place in the next 2 years but only then could the report be seen as having been successful in delivering a framework for making a national infrastructure fit for the 21st century.

That this work, even if not complete, has survived three changes of government and for 10 years highlights its importance; that it has not been fully implemented shows how difficult it can be to change the course of even one element of state provision, particularly when the change proposed is seen as radical. There are continuing challenges to overcome in persuading government to properly adopt a systemic approach to this and other matters.

The pursuit of effectiveness

Functionally arranged organisation structures reflect the ideas of achieving efficiency through division of labour (Smith, 1776; Taylor, 1911), a long history of religious and military structures and growth of science in the Enlightenment with the emergence of individual disciplines and sub-disciplines as bodies of knowledge extended. Through this approach, the state is arguably organised more to demonstrate internal efficiency and control of and accountability for public expenditure, than it is to meet the recognised needs and expectations of citizens. Rooted in outmoded thinking and technology, broad services are provided but are not tailored to individual requirements. Such services may create or enable state dependency because they unintendedly cause a practical or financial trap for the beneficiary and are not as efficient for either provider or beneficiary as they could be. Some attempts to address this through transformation of services, such as Universal Credit in the UK, have not always achieved their objectives[5] nor been uniformly successful for either recipient or provider.[6] While the functional approach to service provision may have been appropriate to the past it is no longer fit for purpose. The market driven, customer focused, information enabled world of 5th generation communications technology and mass availability of data is the 4th industrial revolution and the state lags behind. Commonly, states have not embraced the potential of contemporary technology; they lag behind, under-investing and overspending. Such states are neither economically, socially nor politically viable, so they must not simply do things differently but also do different things; things which empower and enable citizens.

Information technology continues to evolve at a dramatic pace with its technical challenges largely solved or being solved; meanwhile, state organisations have not evolved to process and derive meaning from the exponentially increasing availability of data. Many services operated by or on behalf of the state continue to be producer rather than customer led, providing the illusion of accountability and control yet failing to address citizens' problems or ameliorate their needs. Coupled to that, the history of public sector information systems initiatives, notably but not exclusively in the UK, is discomfiting. Similar concerns can be expressed about infrastructure projects funded by governments; these are often over budget, late and non-performing. Examples in the press include Willy Brandt Brandenburg Airport[7] at Berlin 7 years overdue at the time of writing, the MOSE[8] flood defences in Venice which are 8 years overdue at the time of writing and Crossrail[9] in London 3 years overdue at the time of writing. All examples are also over budget while the 'HS2' railway project in the UK has seen its estimated budget increase from around £36bn to not less than £85bn with some estimates in excess of £100bn. Whether or not that railway can be delivered and generate commensurate economic value and social well-being is being debated. The case makes clear though the challenge of developing a real understanding of value for money from the public purse when an estimate can vary so dramatically. This may especially be the case when that public spending will be made through private sector partners whose primary duty to shareholders is the pursuit of profit and that is not dependent upon project completion.

It may be that governments inhibited and constrained, sometimes by the lack of funding for investment, by political policy, by limited understanding of possibilities, overambitious in scope and with no fallback alternative cannot recognise the emerging potential of technology and act to realise it or benefit from it. Sometimes, they are exploited by private sector organisations but an Intelligent Nation with autonomous citizens and focused on meeting citizens needs might reconcile the need for accountability with the demand for improved performance, localisation and devolution. That new understanding might then inform ways of procuring and providing services which could obviate the sources of errors, delays and frustrations.

The democratic imperative

A country is a single organisation which emerges from the synthesis of its two components: the nation (people, culture, traditions, norms, collective behaviours) and the state (the structure of government and the mechanisms of governance). Nation and state are unified in the UK and some other countries through a set of evolving conventions that we call a constitution while other countries establish their state through a republic with a formal, legally established and relatively fixed constitutional document subject only to clarification through amendment.

Perhaps in an echo of Cartesian dualism, the nation represents the mind, the state represents the body and their synthesis is the country. Government of that country only achieves legitimacy with democratic consent. Consent is the agreement by the people to the processes of management (the activity of governance) and is essential to political sustainability; autocracy cannot be legitimate as it coerces without consent. One difficult challenge when the sources of information and disinformation are beyond their control and, maybe, in some cases their understanding is to ensure that citizen consent is fully informed. We shall return to this later when we consider the idea of a resilient citizen; first we must recognise that public services have perhaps become somewhat detached from their legitimacy.

A country as an organisation necessarily has explicit politics. Those who seek positions of political influence in national or local government do so for the most part in the sincerely held belief that the adoption of their political perspective and their values will improve things for some, or all, of society. Their beliefs, priorities, values and ideas on how social change happens, if supported, become translated into legislation and regulation, taxation, current account spending and investment all arranged to deliver the change or improvement in which they believe.

These political belief systems appear to persist along two continua. The first is commonly posed as a choice between a socialistic economic system and a capitalistic economic system; the second is a choice between totalitarianism (suppression of the individual) and libertarianism (the individual as supreme). Any country reaching the extremes of these continua is unlikely to sustain economic, social or environmental viability. There is a risk that all politics descends into economics because economic well-being is how the value of our beliefs is commonly expressed and applying or withholding it is the means by which power is most often exercised. Money though is a very narrow, asystemic, measure of well-being. Is it a paradox that money does not seem to matter so much when a single-valve failure stops the water flowing[10] or in the Covid-19 pandemic when treasuries worldwide are temporarily absorbing the financial impact of the health crisis?

The issue of governance is different for a country than for other organisations. In a typical organisation, the management is appointed by the owners (however that may be done, whoever that may be) and those owners vest in them the right to manage. For a country that right may be inherited (monarchy), self-appointed (dictatorship) or elected (democracy) or some hybrid and, as Hayek (2006) suggests the first freedom is political, 'the participation of men (sic) in the choice of their government, in the process of legislation, and in the control of administration.'

Each governance archetype has sub-types and significant variance in the way they are achieved. The UK is a constitutional monarchy, it sustains the Sovereign as the Head of State with powers both reserved and limited, while having a bi-cameral parliament in which the members of the lower house (the Commons) are elected on a first past the post basis in each of the 650 constituencies while the members of the upper house (the Lords) are a mix of hereditary and (in effect appointed by politicians) life members. The government is formed, at the invitation of the Sovereign, by the leader of the political party with the greatest number of seats in the Commons. Parliament itself is sovereign in its capacity to make law (Loughlin, 2013) but its continuance in office is at the behest of the citizens through an electoral process. Ultimately in the UK, all power belongs to the individual citizen and is loaned to parliament; government is legitimate when citizens agree it is legitimate!

Across Europe, there are a variety of monarchies and republics while the European Union (EU) is not currently a state in its own right but rather a supra-state membership organisation with membership requiring that countries adhere to treaties which transfer certain powers to the EU to exercise on behalf of all of the Members. While each member country has its own unique constitutional arrangements, their freedoms are to some degree constrained by their membership of the EU. Constituted by treaty between its 27 members, the EU is organised in a number of elements: the Council of Europe (made up of the political leaders of state of the members with a rotating presidency), the European Commission (a European civil service responsible for proposing, formulating and delivering EU policy) and the European Parliament to which members are elected on a proportional representation basis. This method of selection, which allocates seats to parties according to the proportion of votes cast in their favour, breaks the direct link between the individual elector and their local representative. Following a referendum in 2016, the UK Parliament, after prolonged debate which led to much confusion, bitterness and division, passed legislation enabling its withdrawal from membership of the EU which occurred on 31st January 2020. The full ramifications of that decision and the subsequent legislation and withdrawal are unknowable at the time of writing.

In the USA, the President is both Head of State and Head of Government and is appointed through a Presidential election process entirely separate from those which elect the members of the Senate and the House of Representatives. Members of Congress (the lower house has 448 permanent seats) are elected to represent a district (a subset of a state) while the Senate (upper house) has two elected Senators from each state, each representing the whole state. The powers of Congress are limited to those set out in Article One of the United States Constitution[11], all other powers belonging to the states themselves, an explicitly decentralised arrangement on most matters. That constitution, coupled to the evolution of the nation and the passage of time, leaves ample room for interpretation and, as with other countries and constitutional arrangements, there is continuing debate and tension between centralising and decentralising actions.

In every case, there is a system of relatively local government as well as national. The UK, for example, has a Parliament in Scotland with Assemblies in Wales and Northern Ireland, as well as Upper and Lower Tier Local Authorities and, most recently, what are known as 'City Regions' with devolved powers bringing together a number of Authorities under a single Mayor.

In each case, regardless of the detailed arrangements, the tendency of every legislative body is to legislate. Resting on their sincerely held beliefs that there is a better way, each politician seeks to exercise power not just over citizens but over lower-order legislative bodies. The principle of subsidiarity may be applied in some cases, but the higher-order body decides the competences at each level. While the principle of subsidiarity is that each decision should be taken at the lowest level where the competence exists, it is always the higher-order body making the decision about the level of the competences. As De Tocqueville (1835) wrote:

> Decentralization has, not only an administrative value, but also a civic dimension, since it increases the opportunities for citizens to take interest in public affairs; it makes them get accustomed to using freedom. And from the accumulation of these local, active, pernickety freedoms, is born the most efficient counterweight against the claims of the central government, even if it were supported by an impersonal, collective will

The common product of current structures is that more and more power is exercised by fewer and fewer people. When it comes to the determination to devolve power and engage citizens, we find that the Pareto principle does not just apply to the economy but also to electors and their participation in decisions that affect their future. Contrasting with the common trend, Bologna has made an explicit attempt to decentralise and engage its citizens.

Decentralising Bologna: Towards an 'urban commons'?

Bologna[12] has attempted to challenge the process of centralisation and the associated reduction in democracy. Following a decline in citizen engagement and an increase in bureaucracy, the city passed regulation to actively promote engagement by citizens and non-state organisations.

A reformation of local government had created district authorities which mimicked the structure of the overall city authority with commensurate increase in bureaucracy and decrease in engagement with falling trust. In 2014 only 38% of those eligible voted. With a significant non-local and relatively transient population, low political engagement and a challenging bureaucracy, making citizen driven improvement was difficult requiring engagement with multiple functional departments.

The city authority passed legislation in 2014 to permit formal collaboration between the city and citizens, distributing authority for action to reformed districts and allowing utilisation of public spaces and unoccupied buildings, intending through 'local labs' to encourage engagement and connection between local government and citizens with dedicated lead members of staff for each district. The city also established a central hub to oversee the local labs. Coupled to this is a participatory budget process which allows all citizens to engage with and vote on citizen-led projects.

Success was always going to depend on reduction in bureaucracy and design of efficient, effective processes. Citizens prepare proposals which are reviewed through the participatory budgeting process and tested for conflict or support from city wide initiatives and programmes before being voted on by those citizens who choose to engage.

It is reported that by October 2018 around 480 projects had been implemented through this scheme, considered by the city authorities to be successful. The success factors are thought to be the process of engagement, the decentralised decision-making, the trust implied in that decentralisation, the 'hyperlocal' focus and the technical support provided to ensure the best outcomes. With an improving quality of proposal and increasing engagement Bologna is now working to sustain the success.

While this study shows what can be achieved, it also highlights the challenges, particularly the continuing need to balance the freedom of the parts against the constraint of the centre. The decentralising activity required both political will and organisational change which would be difficult to establish and even more so to sustain without a wholesale change of culture. While the system has tolerated this change, it is important to note that the total budget for the work is estimated at around 1 million euros with less than 15,000 people voting from a population reported in 2016 of around 388,000. The experiment does demonstrate how information technology has the potential to make participatory budgeting a more viable, efficient means of public engagement.

It can be argued that some western democracies are drifting towards what feels to some like a totalitarian position, that their governments are losing democratic legitimacy. The hiatus in the UK Parliament at Westminster from 2016 to 2019 provided a prime example of this while the worldwide responses to the Covid-19 pandemic have seen governments award themselves unprecedented powers of pop-ulation control, restriction of movement and work and, critically, powers of surveillance and intervention. Such powers are dangerous in the most benign of hands and it will require the exercise of great democratic power to ensure that they are rolled back at the appropriate time. Whatever the view each elector may have held on the UK remaining in or leaving the EU, Parliament (with the connivance of politicians from all parties and perspectives) offered a choice to the electorate, promised to exercise the choice made and at one stage failed to do so. Any parliament or government placing itself above its electorate, that acts in ways which infringe upon 'political liberties and rights, which is to be regarded as a breach of duty in the ruler' (Mill, 1859) will ultimately suffer.

Each of these systems, and others not described here, has a challenge to its legitimacy. For this argument, and to support the whole idea of an Intelligent Nation, legitimacy of government is an emergent product of the legitimacy of the process by which it is elected and that rests on the extent to which that process is meaningfully democratic.

Democracy and technology: the emerging challenge

In recent years new threats to democracy have emerged from the ability of emergent technologies to provide data to government. Exploring the economic need to use data for the good of all highlights the moral need to protect the citizen from potentially unlimited state interventions and interference made possible through that same data. While the data can transform the notion of state provision through novel and innovative arrangements that serve the citizen rather than the provider, it can equally show the state how to manipulate the citizen (as is already being demonstrated by non-state data providers). Equally, data can be used selectively (Huff, 1991), perhaps disingenuously, to generate answers which suit the protagonists but disguise the inadequacy or failure of that which is reported. There is a need for safeguards and incentives to discourage and prevent data-enabled abuse of power by providers and overdependence by users, an argument for competent and reasonable data usage by the state on behalf of the citizen. While a public sector work ethos of service not exploitation may provide a safe cultural fit, the need to protect the citizen from the predations of the state and the technology companies cannot be ignored especially when private companies are contracted to provide public services.

The function of any information system is to provide information for decision-making. The value of that information rests in its contribution to the personal viability of each citizen and in its usefulness to comprehension by the state of citizens' needs. An Intelligent Nation should draw on Beer's (1979) idea of the neuro-cybernetic model of organisation, the information system as a 'nervous system'. Pervading the state, the importance, security and the rights and obligations of government and citizens in the capture, security and use of data need deep consideration. Just because something can be done that does not mean that it should be; as Wiener (1948) suggested, the emergence of new science 'embraces technical developments with great possibilities for good and for evil'. While technology itself may be considered by some as morally blind its application by humans and, increasingly, by artificially intelligent systems is fraught with risks of good and evil, with possibilities of use and abuse, some visible, some not, some intended, some not. Transparency by, of and for government in data collection, storage, manipulation and use will be an essential component in maintaining the freedom of the citizen and of democracy; our current systems and thinking are insufficient to provide the necessary protections.

The Intelligent Nation: A transformation

The Intelligent Nation demands an outcome-oriented, citizen-centred state focused on meeting the evolving lifetime needs of the citizen. It proposes a transformational shift in focus from the provision of inputs to the achievement of outcomes. It recognises that the greatest achievement of the state should be to increase its value to citizens by maximising their independence and reducing their need for reliance on it. Organisational systems, whether state or private, are purposeful to the extent that they contribute to the achievement of desired outcomes. When state systems are not fulfilling the citizens' purpose, they are serving themselves and, beyond that set of value enabling activities essential to their continued survival, anything that they do can be considered as 'muda' (Ohno, 1988) or waste.

A change is needed in the arrangements for the provision of social (public services) and fundamental (utilities) infrastructure to enable fulfilment of purpose. An Intelligent Nation rests not on a binary politico-economic choice between 'nationalised or not' 'state-provided or not' but on a systemic radical transformation of the organisation, management and performance of the services the state provides to its citizens. This must capitalise on the potential offered by contemporary information capability to support the rights and obligations both to and of citizens. To be clear, just changing the ownership model is not the answer; as has been seen with the nationalisation and later privatisation of utilities while some aspects improve, others deteriorate; the system needs change. The fear, as Hayek (2006) suggests, is that 'We are not far from that point where the deliberately organized forces of society may destroy those forces which have made advance possible'. An Intelligent Nation will be adaptive, will learn to systemically synthesise the whole of state provision of services through the multiple lenses of citizen outcomes, process, behaviour and information in parallel. Giving primacy to none, an Intelligent Nation would seek the optimal dynamic balance, proposing transformation based on the citizens' demand rather than production push.

The transformation required exists in three parts.

First is that the governance (in the UK that is The Houses of Parliament, Local Authorities, Statutory and Regulatory bodies) of it all needs to sustain democratic legitimacy through the informed consent of an engaged population. It must be oriented around social, environmental or economic sustainability. The whole must be designed as an adaptive system, driving up performance and driving down cost over time. The measure of success in governance and public services may be best understood by the reduction in need for them, that is, they are most successful when they are least required.

Second is the need to recognise that much of the activity of the state (tax assessment and collection, social welfare collections and payments, licenses, permissions, documents) is grounded in rule-based information processing which can be done more reliably, consistently, efficiently and effectively by digital technology than it can by people. There must be a digital revolution to enhance provision and reduce costs simultaneously.

Third is that those services which are dependent on high-quality human interaction, for example, healthcare, education, social care, military, policing and justice, must be customer oriented, designed for and driven by the achievement of citizen-focused outcomes. Resources released from the second change can be redeployed to support this.

Transformation of the state is a response to contemporary challenges, opportunities and unrealised potential. The challenges include overcoming the continually increasing centralisation of power inherent in bureaucratic systems; the functional orientation of state activities and the difficulties that approach imposes on citizens; the pursuit of effectiveness; the growing democratic deficit and the consequences for the legitimacy of state activity.

Summary

The argument so far is that the nation (the people of any country) are ill-served by a centralising, change smothering, non-adaptive bureaucracy that organisationally, technologically and culturally fails to keep pace with the evolution of its wider society. To be viable, resilient, survival worthy, every nation must address the democratic deficit, grasp the challenges of supranational organisations and learn to blend a capitalistic capability to generate value with a socialistic capability to ensure its distribution to achieve equitable outcomes. The challenges this presents are pursued in the rest of this book.

This will require a transformation based on a cybernetically informed model embracing an information-based hierarchy and highly decentralised decision-making, the Intelligent Nation. The principles of Intelligent Organisation will enable a resilient state from governance through civil and military administration while weaknesses and flaws in the current functional orientation will be addressed. Considering the relationship between the individual and the state means thinking about what makes a citizen resilient, their needs, values, skills and behaviours and how public services need to be arranged to support them. A new model of engagement is needed based on a citizen-centred model of state provision.

The overall structure of services, newly arranged around the varying needs at different life stages, must be redesigned to maximise the value of support while minimising the disruption to the individual. The focus of design must be first on understanding those services that the State provides to all citizens equally, regardless of need and second, how the needs and desires of individual citizens can be met through services and systems that deliver tailored outcomes. A particular need is to look at the cost and value of provision from a systemic perspective, taking account of the total cost of provision including those imparted to the citizen.

When we understand the outcomes required for citizens, we can view the provision of infrastructure and utilities. This requires consideration of the strengths and weaknesses of the current means of provision relative to needs and the economic, social, climate and systemic risks inherent in the current situation. Alternative business models must be explored, challenging the current blend of private, public and hybrids to resolve long-term challenges including proposing an alternative ownership model rooted in community participation in ownership.

Finally, we must critique the current means and methods of performance reporting and management before proposing a radical new model based on the idea that any nation needs to be an explicitly adaptive system. If any nation is to survive, it must both support and empower its citizens, balance state and individual spending and, over time, achieve harmony between citizens and state over social and economic priorities and preferences.

The Intelligent Nation offers the opportunity to transform the organisation and provision of public services of all types and at all levels of localisation while sustaining a legitimate government founded on active, engaged democracy. Transformation must not be stifled by self-preserving, self-interested, cautious, creeping incrementalism but enabled by a radical and revolutionary embrace of the contemporary potential of people and process driven by information.

Key points

- The Intelligent Nation is a synthesis of people (who are the nation) and the state (the system of government and governance);
- The current inefficient, bureaucratic, centralised producer-driven arrangements will not suffice; there must be a reassertion of citizen autonomy;
- The structure of the state and its delivery arrangements are non-adaptive;
- The state must be organised around the citizen and their needs not functional accountability; they need to pursue effectiveness not just efficiency;
- States must sustain social and fundamental infrastructure but is failing to keep up with the needs of the nation;
- States have evolved not been designed; an adaptive systemic understanding and approach is needed;
- Transformation must be exploiting the capability of technology to deliver radically redesigned services and underpinning infrastructure rooted in an engaged population giving democratic legitimacy to government and governance.

References

Ackoff, R.L., (1981) *Creating the Corporate Future*, Wiley, New York

Beckford, J., (1994) Entropy and Entrepreneurship: The Centralisation of Capital as a Barrier to Innovatory Behaviour, *Entrepreneurship, Innovation and Change*, 3 (1), Plenum, New York

Beer, S., (1979) *The Heart of Enterprise*, Wiley, Chichester

Beer, S., (1993) 'World in Torment: A Time Whose Idea Must Come,' Presidential Address to the Triennial Conference of the World Organisation of Systems and Cybernetics, New Delhi, India

Council for Science and Technology, (2009) *An Infrastructure for the 21st Century*, HMSO, London, UK

De Tocqueville, A., (1835–1840) *Democracy in America*, Saunders and Otley, London

Friedman, M., (1982) *Capitalism and Freedom*, University of Chicago Press, Chicago, USA

Hayek, F.A., (2006) *The Constitution of Liberty*, Routledge Classics, London

Huff, D., (1991) *How to Lie with Statistics*, Penguin, London

Loughlin, M., (2013) *The British Constitution*, Oxford University Press, Oxford

Mill, J.S., (1859) *On Liberty*, Parker and Son, London (Pelican Classics, 1974)

Ohno, T., (1988) *Toyota Production System*, Productivity Press, New York

Pugh, D.S. & Hickson, D.J., (1989) *Writers on Organisations*, Penguin, London

Sampson, A., (1993) *The Essential Anatomy of Britain*, Coronet, London

Smith, A., (1776/1991) *The Wealth of Nations*, Everyman edition, Random Century, London.

Taylor, F., (1911) *The Principles of Scientific Management*, The Plimpton Press, Norwood, MA

Weber, M., (1924) 'Legitimate authority and bureaucracy,' in *Organisation Theory, Selected Readings*, D.S. Pugh (ed.), 3rd edition, 1990, Penguin, London

Wiener, N., (1948) *Cybernetics: Or Control and Communication in the Animal and the Machine*, The Massachusetts Institute of Technology, Boston, MA

Notes

1. https://www.telegraph.co.uk/news/2017/08/21/mod-fails-cut-civilians-help-fill-30bn-defence-black-hole/ 30/12/2019
2. https://nhsfunding.info/symptoms/10-effects-of-underfunding/rationing/ 30/12/2019
3. https://www.independent.co.uk/news/uk/crime/met-police-spending-cuts-400-million-funding-london-crimes-not-investigated-burglary-assault-a8002746.html 30/12/2019
4. https://www.ukcric.com/ 30/12/2019
5. https://www.bbc.co.uk/news/uk-politics-47203389 30/12/2019
6. https://www.ohchr.org/Documents/Issues/Poverty/EOM_GB_16Nov2018.pdf 30/12/2019
7. https://edition.cnn.com/travel/article/berlin-brandenburg-airport-debacle/index.html 15/11/2019
8. https://www.newcivilengineer.com/latest/delayed-mose-defence-would-have-prevented-venice-flooding-01-11-2018/ 15/12/2019
9. https://www.bbc.co.uk/news/business-47967766 15/12/2019
10. https://www.itv.com/news/2019-12-14/thousands-left-without-water-supply-due-to-damaged-valve/ 15/12/2019
11. https://www.archives.gov/founding-docs/constitution-transcript 31/12/2019
12. https://citiesofservice.org/resource/co-creating-urban-commons-bologna-italy 27/12/2019

2

SUSTAINABLE AND RESILIENT STATE

Introduction

If any country is to be intelligent, viable, sustainable and resilient, it must adopt structures, activities and behaviours which deliver those outcomes. The Intelligent Organisation (Beckford, 2020), developed using cybernetic principles, is concerned with just these mechanisms. The language of cybernetics is useful for describing a country as a complex adaptive system with two primary sub-systems: the nation (people) and the state (all aspects of government and governance). The ideas of cybernetics provide a framework through which the principles of a state designed to meet the expectations set out at the end of the previous chapter can be met.

Principles of Intelligent Organisation

An Intelligent Organisation is adaptive, using information about itself and its environment to achieve 'allostasis' (Beckford, 2020) or 'ultra-stability' (Ashby, 1956), that is, systemic dynamic stability. This requires adaptive processes and learning behaviours to be designed into the fabric of the organisation to enable effective response to unforeseen or unexpected events. Given that, as Beer suggested, 'the cybernetics will assert themselves', then they should be designed to support the desired outcomes including intended purposes. Any such adaptive system adheres to four principles (adapted from Beckford, 1993):

> **The Systems Principle**: any system taken as a whole has emergent properties; composed of sub-systems, it displays characteristics as a whole system that are not found in any of its parts. An example of this is flight; a property that can be found in a whole aircraft (airframe, propulsion system, control system and pilot) but not in any of its parts. In an organisation an emergent property might be culture or morale; they arise from the interactions of the people,

systems and environment but are not a component of any. Deconstructing the system dissipates the emergent properties.

The Black Box Principle: any exceedingly complex system cannot be completely known. We learn to manage it by methodical study of the manipulation of its inputs, studying and codifying the consequent outputs. Any large organisation is exceedingly complex and while its elements, both material and incorporeal, may be knowable, the extent and range of interactions between them is not. We can only learn how any organisation really works by observing its behaviour (Beckford, 2020). We must deal with the system as a whole since its behaviour belongs only to that whole system.

The Principle of Self-Regulation: any complex, dynamical system will demonstrate self-regulation resulting from internal and external information exchanges. The dynamics of its internal relationships will generate equilibrium with its environment and that will be sustained while the level of energy is sufficient and external perturbations are within the limits of system resilience. Managers must comprehend the self-regulating circular causal processes in order to intervene effectively. Inappropriately timed or directed interventions may induce undesired instability or perturbation.

The Law of Requisite Variety (Ashby, 1956): regulation of any system can only be competent when the regulator has as much capacity to generate variety (the number of states or conditions it can exhibit) as the system to be regulated. Requisite here means necessary. Dynamical systems, incompletely known or understood, demonstrate behaviours that appear, at least in part, to be random; they are probabilistic rather than deterministic. Variety engineering enables the management of that probabilism through structural, planning and control activities. These include decision autonomy, delegation, setting objectives, generating behavioural norms and rules, that is, the conscious inculcation of a preferred culture or ways of working. A critical component of organisations as complex adaptive systems is people, who bring to bear knowledge, insight, expertise and experience which amplify its capability.

Dealing with an organisation and the outcomes of its activities as a systemic whole demands acceptance that some elements are unknowable, using information to enable both self-regulation (stability) and managerial decision-making (adaptation). To achieve a sustained change in the organisation will mean changing the information, the behaviour and the structural arrangements so that adaptiveness becomes inherent. Such change will alter the emergent properties of the system.

The effective manager, the steersman or governor, must address three problems simultaneously:

Problem 1: Managing the Present – How to do things better;

Problem 2: Creating the Future – How to do better things;

Problem 3: Nurturing Identity – Defining 'better'.

Ashby (1956) wrote that 'Cybernetics … treats, not things but *ways of behaving*' while Beer (1979, 1981, 1985), developing the Viable System Model (VSM) from first principles, offered what has commonly been interpreted as a somewhat technocratic, structural model of a survival-worthy organisation. For me, that interpretation is rooted in a very limited comprehension of Beer's work, belonging more to the observers (his critics) than to the VSM and the underpinning ideas. While Beer's concern for society and human well-being is most easily discoverable and accessible through the discourse in 'Designing Freedom' (1974), consideration of the principles of the VSM makes it clear that the model is both structural and behavioural. In the synthesis of those two dimensions rests the essence of systemic viability for organisations. Adherence to the principles of the VSM requires the development of a genuinely shared identity between the governed and the governors, the leaders and the led. That shared identity, a common sense of purpose, both generated by and generating a flow of information is essential to the closure of the structural logic of the model and equally critical to the legitimacy and therefore the sustainability of the processes of governance. The VSM, from which the idea of the model of the Intelligent Organisation is developed, demands that a legitimate process underpin its governance and its governance must underpin fulfilment of purpose.

Purpose, identity and legitimate governance

Thinking about the state as an Intelligent Organisation arguably starts with Plato's (390BC) idea of the steersman, steering the ship of state, a founding metaphor of 'kybernetes' (cybernetics) or governance. This captures the essence of an Intelligent Nation, working with clarity of purpose, intent and identity, directing itself toward a desired future in a dynamic environment. The destination cannot be the notionally fixed target of Plato's steersman (cybernetician) but rather one which evolves: pursuit of a continually improving outcome measured by increasing proximity to fulfilment of purpose. The implication of this is that the organisational system is evolving both at the operational level (making progress towards a current target) and at the meta-system (governance) level. It is adapting to improve performance while simultaneously redefining what performance means.

The purpose of any system is the reason for which it exists. In the Intelligent Nation, the definition of that purpose must belong to the citizens and be pursued by them and by government on their behalf; it is a joint enterprise and must be shared. Beer argued that the purpose of a system is to be itself, that is, that any living (dynamic) system pursues its own survival and in doing so becomes treatable as a viable system. It uses information about itself and its environment to adapt and is evolutionary in pursuit of its own existence. For an Intelligent Nation, the state must be the servant of purpose, created by the citizens to act for them and on their behalf, the means by which their will is delivered.

To treat a system as both discrete (bounded) and purposeful (acting with intent) requires determining what is part of the system and what is exogenous, an environmental influence. The boundary of a human being or an animal is clear; they have for all practical purposes a physical boundary (setting aside epiphytic, parasitic and symbiotic systems in which we identify the two bounded elements but recognise that one cannot live without the other). All dynamical systems, to some extent, exist interdependently with their environment and drawing the usually porous boundary between the two is the subject of much debate. Boundary critique (Ulrich, 1983) acknowledges that judgements about systems depend on evaluations of what facts and norms should be included or excluded from consideration. In organisations we can define certain things as being within the legally bounded system, that is, the limits of its legal personality, while for countries the limits extend to rights of self-governance and judicial power. Such physical and political boundaries though are permeable, transcended by international treaties, memberships and organisations generating superordinate regulatory systems. Global markets now contain numerous corporations whose economic size and scope is vastly greater than that of some countries in which they trade; can they still be treated as subject to the political and judicial boundaries of the countries that host them? They surely must be if governments are to fulfil their functions.

There is a primary difference between the intelligent non-governmental organisation and the intelligent state. In the first the legitimacy of governance is a function of the membership of the organisation. Appointed by the members (commonly shareholders, partners, trustees, employees), management is authorised to conduct its affairs within the law and powers delegated to them by the members. The legitimacy of decisions rests in legal compliance and the delegated authority, employees may choose to follow such legitimate instructions or, in a viable organisation (which requires that choices can be exercised) to work elsewhere. What employees cannot do is change the management; that prerogative is reserved to members. Managers are bound by law to act in the best interests of the owners. This can lead them to engage in activities (such as short-term profit maximisation) which may be oppressive to the employees or damaging to the medium or long-term viability of the organisation. However, in making the organisation serve only short-term or narrowly defined objectives, they may impair its viability, Deming (1986) discusses this saying:

> Anyone can boost the dividend at the end of the quarter. Ship everything on hand, regardless of quality: mark it shipped, and show it all as accounts receivable. Defer till next quarter, so far as possible, orders for material and equipment. Cut down on research, education, training.

The illusion of success is briefly sustained while the viability of the organisation is threatened; readers will be able to cite their own examples of companies which have pursued this approach.

By contrast, the legitimacy of government is at the behest of the citizen. There is tension between the legitimate right and obligation to govern in the interests of all the people and the legitimate right and obligation of each individual to exercise their freedom, in particular their collective freedom to change the government. In choosing to have a particular government, each citizen in a democracy relinquishes some degree of self-determination; autonomy is constrained but by consent of those constrained. We choose to constrain ourselves.

When applying the ideas to national or local government, sustainability requires that the identity and purpose be held in common by the governors and the governed. The legitimacy of any government is a function of the process by which it is created and if the government is to be sustainable, then the members of the state, the citizens, who define the nation (Hobsbawm, 1990), must have the ability to change it. In the UK the complexity is amplified by the establishment of the Church of England which, in law, seeks to unite the 'official' Church and the State, most visibly through the role of the monarch as both Head of State and Head of Church, 'the Defender of the Faith'.

Nurturing identity: Rev. Keith Elford

The Intelligent Organisation nurtures its identity so that it is able to arbitrate with integrity between the claims of the present and the future. If one applies this thought to the United Kingdom, and especially to England, then one is bound to consider how national identity is formed and nurtured. In particular, I want to consider the role of the Church of England in establishing and maintaining that identity. Given the decline in that church, measured by attendance and influence what is the impact on national identity?

Our history, like that of the European continent as a whole, is the history of a society shaped by the church, intertwined with the state. In the Medieval period the Roman Catholic Church wielded immense economic, religious, moral, social and political power across the continent. After the reformation, in most cases, the reformed countries maintained the concept of a national church and of state sponsored faith – though now it was the princes who wielded the greater power. As is well-known, the proximate cause of the English reformation was Henry VIII's dispute with the Pope over his desire to divorce and remarry. But this rejection of the authority of the Pope was probably related to a burgeoning sense of national identity, and with it a desire for national independence, felt across western Europe, including in England (Ryrie, 2016: (41). In the aftermath of the Elizabethan settlement the Church of England became completely embedded in the life of the nation, playing a key role in education, in rites of passage, and in the political establishment – at the heart of its life and identity. To be baptised was 'as much a mark of Englishness as of Christian conviction' (Davie, 2016: 295). The emerging non-conformist movements (later, denominations) were seen initially as rivals (MacCulloch, 2009) but the Church of England learned to live alongside them. This dispensation went through many challenges and changes (the Civil War, the rise of science, continental revolutions, the declining influence of Anglicanism in Scotland, Wales and Ireland, for example) but it seemed clear until quite recently that the UK was a Christian country with the Church of England as the primary expression of that fact.

Changes were quietly taking place, however. According to the British Social Attitudes survey 'church attendance has declined steadily since at least 1851, when a government count showed about half the population, then about 5.3 million, in church on a particular Sunday'. The decline has been sharp since the 1960s: today there only about 722,000 people in Church of England services on a Sunday (Curtice et al., 2019: 3). It is in this latter period, from the 1960s, that talk of 'post-Christendom' has become commonplace. We are no longer a Christian country in the sense that we were.

No doubt many welcome this change. The Church of England can be seen as an institution which has connived with oppression, fanned the flames of jingoism (notably in its role in the First World War: see MacCulloch, 2009: 917) and been identified with the forces of conservatism. It has no place, certainly no privileged role, in a multi-cultural, progressive society in which a high value is placed on freedom. It is all too clearly identified with the forces of traditionalism, of out-moded social patterns and expectations inimical to the contemporary pursuit of the authentic self (Taylor, 2007). Contemporary debates within the church about sexuality no doubt add to this impression – that of a church woefully out of touch. But is that really the whole story?

Perhaps we should first consider more carefully what we might mean when we speak of a church being at the heart of national identity. It is not necessary for the church to be established to have that kind of influence, as the example of the United States shows. But it does have a particular history and shape in the UK which is strongly linked with establishment. In the first place we might note that the parochial system embeds the Church of England 'into the physical and cultural landscape' (Davie, 2016: 290). But perhaps even more significant is the influence of the church on our 'social imaginary', that is, our way of seeing and understanding the world (Taylor, 2007). We see evidence of this still, perhaps, in two features of modern British life. The first is that, although there are fewer churchgoers, communities appear to value their churches and the continuation of its rituals (Davie, 2016: 290). Secondly, there is a great deal of public interest in the Church of England – in its debates on sexuality, for example. This may well indicate that the British people still view the church as an arena in which 'society as a whole comes to terms with profound shifts in the moral climate' (Davie, 2016: 291). To me it is striking that the sharpest decline in the Church of England's fortunes has taken place at roughly the same time that UK has been working out the consequences of the loss of empire and of superpower status. For many commentators the desire for Brexit is a symptom of the identity crisis this latter phenomenon is held to have prompted (see e.g. O'Toole, 2018). But perhaps the sense of a national desire to regain a lost identity is also related to the decline in the Church of England's influence. Perhaps the nostalgic reaching for old models of national identity (and for Brexit) is not only driven by the desire to hark back to the era when UK 'won two world wars' but one where there was a stronger moral and social order of which the church was a key part.

The Church of England has not, of course, been an unmitigated 'good thing'. Its history, like that of all churches, is marred by (sometimes egregious) failures to live up to the example of Christ himself. But, on the other hand, if we believe that all human beings are precious and essentially equal, that love is the supreme value and that a civilised society is one which cares for all, especially the weak, then it is the Christian tradition we have to thank (Hart, 2009). And the Church of England remains an active player on the national and local scene. It still just about maintains a presence in all communities. It is still there when many other agencies are not. It provides public buildings of beauty and peace. It gives a home to other community groups in its church halls. For the most part it witnesses to a generous and affirming form of Christianity. It provides what someone called 'serious space for serious thought', a rare commodity in 21st century UK. The Church of England still provides a very high number of the nation's volunteers. And, for all its conservatism, the Church of England has not only supported and affirmed what are sometimes called 'family values', it has also, sometimes at least, held before us the more ambitious ethic of the gospels – that we are not just to love our families, but also our neighbours and even, our enemies. Sometimes we have been reminded of what UK might be called to be – a place where the kingdom of God is active, where justice reigns and 'Jerusalem is builded here, in this green and pleasant land.' Though one must acknowledge that Blake might have had the conservatism of the Church of England in his sights in his original poem (!), I think I am justified in quoting Jerusalem with reference to the more radical spirits who have also made their home in that church. In fact, the genius of the Church of England has been to provide an example of how opposing views can not only co-exist, more or less peaceably, but find a positive, innovative and holistic resolution within the larger framework provided by the Christian faith (Avis, 2008: 29).

Today, as any parish priest can tell you, most people, and certainly most young people, not only do not go to church, they know very little about it. There is a cadre of militant atheists (Richard Dawkins being the most well-known) but most people are not hostile to faith and the church – the Church of England, and the churches in general, are simply not part of their world. Many more people now identify as non-religious in surveys. 'In 1983... two-thirds of the British public identified as Christian. This figure now stands at just over one third (38%) with 52% of the public saying they do not regard themselves as belonging to any religion' (Curtice et al., 2019: 5). It is not clear that the Church of England will continue to be valued even in the vicarious role it currently plays for many. The Church of England remains, for now, intertwined with government but the arguments for disestablishment may grow. Meanwhile, as the Brexit debate has indicated, we seem a people uncertain and divided about who we are. The importance of identity suggests there are questions for our society that will require some answers if we are to move into the future in a way that is likely to be sustainable. If we wish to discard the Church of England, where will we look for a contemporary source of identity? How will we deal with the heritage that has undoubtedly shaped us? And there is a big question for the Church of England. Can it adapt to the changes in the world around it and contribute positively (though likely differently) to the identity of UK in the future?

Citizens perhaps need devices such as churches and political parties, as enablers of shared identity and beliefs and a sense of belonging, yet each time a boundary is created somebody is excluded. We need parties, churches, societies, networks and clubs to promote our sense of belonging, but such belonging both includes and excludes.

Any government that seeks to sustain its position without popular consent will do so either at great economic or social cost or, more likely, both. The economic cost will be realised through lower economic growth and a higher cost of maintaining order, the social cost through the ongoing need to limit or suppress the aspirations of the population[1] and the consequent loss of enterprising activity. Effective democracy requires a continuing meaningful dialogue between governed and government, it cannot simply rely on a periodic electoral process generating an onslaught of promises designed to secure votes, a client nation. If there is a democratic deficit there is no proper foundation for the activities of the state. History is littered with examples of non-democratic or power biased regimes with inequalities of engagement and participation reflected in inequality of opportunity for those in society with the least of everything (UNDP, 2019). In such constrained conditions the lack of competitive drive for efficiency, combined with central planning and costly methods of maintaining social discipline such as those employed in the Chinese system of Social-Credit (Yan, 2019) and other more onerous methods of policing behaviour, has led to reduced economic surpluses and limited demand for goods and services. This may then lead to unwillingness or fear in exchanging ideas dampening any sense of belongingness or shared identity. The following vignette highlights how life changes with a changing comprehension of freedom and sense of self.

An immigrant's reflection: Anonymous

An immigrant leaves many dimensions of self at the country of birth with the hope that many other selves would thrive and flourish.

Growing up in a country where religion is entwined with politics, it was difficult to have the opportunity of questioning ideologies and beliefs, even more so, when the exposure to diverse opinions is limited. I moved to Ireland the day after my master's viva. With the pressure of defending my thesis and getting ready to travel over 3,000 miles away from home for the first time, I did not have the opportunity to really appreciate how big this step was, until I sat on the plane and thought to myself this is it! Living with parents for 24 years, now travelling to another side of the world, where the difference in the daily spoken language was just one of the many on the list!

You leave your first self when you step on the plane. On paper, you are still a member of the family, the eldest child but realistically, you are not part of their life anymore. You miss small events first then big events get into the mix. You would not have the luxury of seeing your family frequently and your role as eldest child and sister now significantly diminishes. I was (and still am) the first member of the family and the very first female in my extended family to leave the country for further higher education. With this background, every step of the journey was my very first experience: shopping on my own, renting a place to live, signing contacts, managing bills and finance, with the constant worry that if for any reason my expenditure got out of ordinary or I faced any problem I will not have the luxury of calling my parents to help me out in a matter of hours.

The first instinct, when you are so far from home, is to search for reminders of home (starting with the same language) so you could satisfy some elements of the lost self. The danger of this instinct is that you lose time in getting integrated into the new surroundings, which defeats the purpose of migrating in the first place. Personally, I think this is the first indication that defines the success of migration with all the sacrifices that it entails. This is where you decide not to see yourself as an outsider anymore and stop using 'them' and 'us' in the daily conversations. This is where you start calling the place you 'chose' to live 'home', taking an interest in current affairs, learning the values, understanding political systems, exercising your rights as an equal(ish) citizen and getting your voice heard in a truly democratic system. Now this, for a woman from a middle-eastern country, where exercising trivial personal decisions such as clothing is heavily prescribed, is a remarkable experience. This is where you grow a self-respecting, self-reliant and confident dimension.

When you grow up in the country that from the highest level of authority to smallest communities have diminishing views and ideologies about women's role in society, it is inevitable that you would start feeling that you are a second-class citizen. You would stop seeing yourself as equal and naturally give up on demanding equal rights at work and society as a whole. This is why, when you get the opportunity to have (almost) equal rights to men in a society, you would grab that opportunity with all your might and never let go. This is when you would not miss a chance of casting your vote even in the most local community elections.

Apart from getting an opportunity of exercising the rights that you were stripped off at the country that you were born and grew up in, migration gives an incredible perception of the world. On this side of the world, the scale of issues and the headlines are on an entirely different level. Yes, there are still issues with abortion laws and you would worry about Brexit's impact but on the other side [in my birth country], a woman's life is considered equal to half of a man and you are not even given the opportunity of expressing your views on the utterly discriminating rules.

Being from a generation who recalls the dial-up connections and the thrill of the connecting to the outside world despite heavy filters, you would extremely appreciate the opportunity of living in a country where having access to the internet is considered a human right, let alone having access to all sorts of news media and social platforms.

With the recent plane crash, all I can think of is the lost unlived lives. All those who went through many difficulties and jumped through many hoops to live a different life for themselves and secure a better future for the next generation. Now all is gone with an 'unintentional human error'. People who made sacrifices, left their families, friends and loved ones behind with the hope that maybe they can get an opportunity to taste freedom in thinking, in the way of living and some certainty for their future.

Reflecting on this insight, perhaps true identity can only be discovered when the individual is placed in a different context or environment, one in which they must choose for themselves the things they will believe in, the rules they will accept, the constraints that they will not. That will require them to learn, reflect and adapt, to use information about their experience of living to modify their way of being themselves.

Integration by design

The Intelligent Organisation is integrated by design; that design synthesises people, their behaviours and skills with processes to achieve outcomes for which it is rewarded by its environment (Dudley, 1998) in the form of energy which, in the organisational case, is information. Most critical in its adaptive capability is that of ideation or origination; the truly Intelligent Organisation is capable of adaptation to circumstances that were not, indeed could not be, envisaged by its designers. Critically, the capacity for true ideation rests with its human actors.

Embedded in its environment, an Intelligent Organisation (Figure 2.1) consists of an informational integration of processes, systems and decisions synthesised by human actors through the application of their values, behaviours and skills and directed towards the achievement of a purposeful and shared outcome. Performance

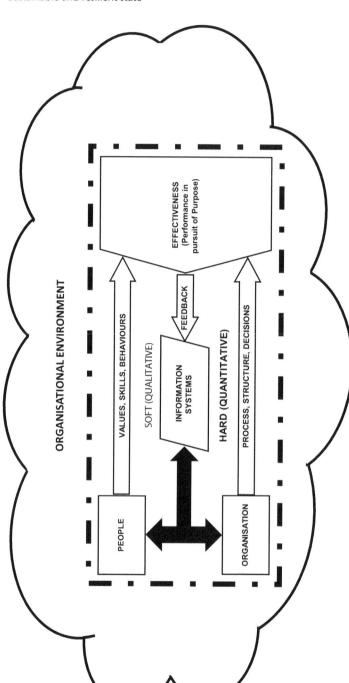

FIGURE 2.1 Intelligent organisation in its environment

is expressed as effectiveness in achieving that outcome. If Beer (1985) was right and 'the purpose of the system is what its does' then performance means alignment of outcome and identity; 'I do what I do because I am who I am'.

The outcome gives external legitimacy to the persistence of the organisation in its environment while purposefulness gives internal legitimacy to the activities themselves. Actions which do not contribute to the fulfilment of purpose or the adaptation of the organisation to enable its autopoiesis (self-production) are pathological, indicative of disease or disorder.

An Intelligent Organisation is comprised of four distinctive sub-systems which are:

Value–Generating Processes: those which produce the outputs valued by the customers of the organisation. All such processes must be designed as self-regulating, containing activities which enable their own stability and localised adaptation; the governance activities that we usually call 'management'. Being both purposeful and self-regulating these are intelligent organisations in their own right.

Value–Enabling Processes: those which are undertaken on behalf of the organisation as a whole which explore opportunities and challenges in its environment and stimulate systemic adaptation. All such processes are again self-regulating, containing management activities, but they are only purposeful to the extent that they contribute to the viability of the whole organisation.

The Trialogue: is a synthesising structure (Dudley, 2000), the meta-systemic mechanism whereby the tension between the present (do things better) and the future (do better things) is resolved by reference to the identity of the organisation (defining 'better'). That tension exists because the value-generating processes work within existing constraints, pursuing productivity. The value-enabling processes are informed by a view of the evolving needs of the environment and the demands it makes for the future, they are pursuing opportunity. The tension is resolved by reference to 'identity', to the need or opportunity in the environment the organisation seeks to address. That identity is an emergent expression of the values, beliefs, hopes and expectations of the human actors that constitute the organisation. This makes it clear why there must be consistency in gubernatorial actions and a shared identity between those who lead and those who are led.

An Integrating Information System: Consisting of both 'soft' and 'hard' information. The first reflects the values of the actors, their belief system, their ways of behaving and is transmitted through human interaction. The second consists of the quantified and verifiable data reflecting the formal processes of the organisation while the information system connects the whole. Considered as the nervous system of the organisation in the 'neuro-cybernetic' perspective (Clemson, 1984), this enables communication and decision and is the information infrastructure on which the organisation depends for its existence.

These four elements can be brought together in a single representation (see Figure 2.2).

The organisation must be designed backwards from the needs and desires of current customers in the current technology and market environment through the value-generating processes. The value-enabling processes explore the needs, desires and opportunities generated by its future customers in the evolving problematic (because it is uncertain and probabilistic) environment. It resolves the tension between the alternative possibilities presented by these environments through the trialogue (Dudley, 2000). This (Figure 2.3) synthesises the information flows into simulations of possible futures; choices between them are informed by reference to the purpose of the organisation which is informed by the values and beliefs of the human actors.

Observant readers will have noted that the structure of the whole model is replicated in each of the value-generating processes. This is because each of those system elements, to be viable, must be both purposeful and competent to function independently of the whole and such competence requires a meta-system, that is, a local management capability. This requirement also helps us discern which processes should be treated as value generating and which as value enabling. It is evident that a structurally recursive and information-based hierarchy is emerging; the whole system contains sub-systems which are themselves whole systems contained within the higher order model. The whole system has a different insight to the environment of the organisation than do its contained systems; it has different information and can make different decisions. This generates a logical and informational hierarchy rather than one rooted in positional power, a hierarchy in which the actors with the most useful information relative to the task, problem or challenge, have the power to make the decision.

Gödel (1929) proposed that within the limits of any formal language some propositions are undecidable and can only be resolved by reference to a higher order language. When we consider an organisation, we can suggest that an embedded value-generating process will encounter propositions which, within the limits of its operating freedoms and its delegated powers, are undecidable and must be referred to the containing or meta-system for decision. In any relationship (personal or business) the parties will have, more or less explicitly, reached an understanding of actions and decisions that may be taken by each individual. When a circumstance arises in which one of the parties is confronted by a decision that falls outside the agreement then, behaving consistently, they will refer the matter to the particular whole system (the relationship is a system that contains the individual parties). Failure to do so would have consequences for the continuance of the relationship. We must not just accept that information-based hierarchy will emerge but that it is logically necessary to the sustainability of any organisation. To be consistent with all power belonging to the individual, there must be rules for managing and sustaining their autonomy. Those rules must be made by those affected, either directly or via representatives whose continuation in that position they can influence. The constrained must agree with the constraints if the whole system is to be intelligent in its behaviour and capability.

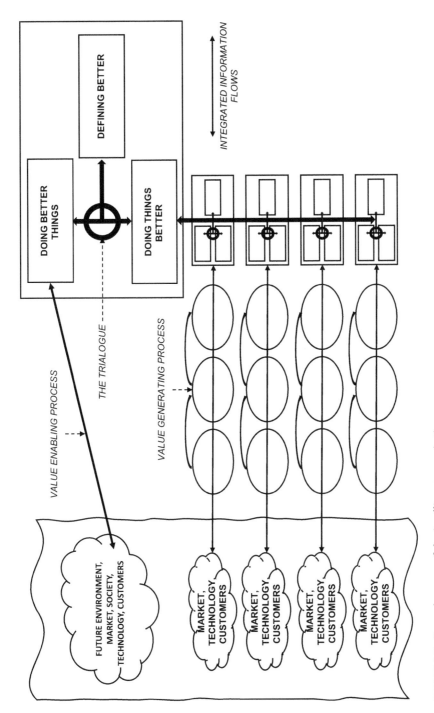

FIGURE 2.2 Four elements of the intelligent organisation

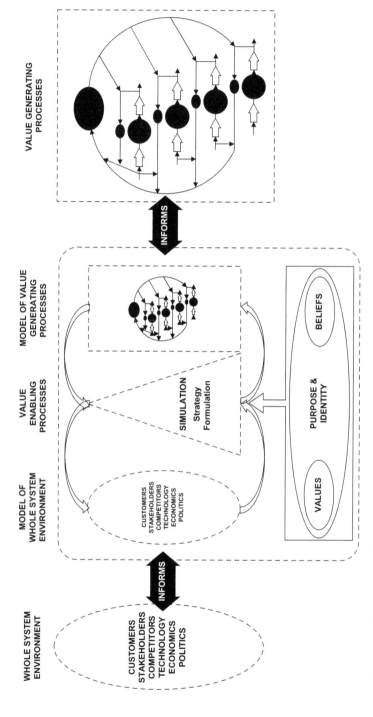

FIGURE 2.3 The trialogue (alternative presentation)

Autonomy

Earlier it was suggested that legitimacy of government in a democratic state rests in the ability of the people to change that government; the ultimate product of applied autonomy. Managing autonomy is the mechanism that sustains the persistent compromises between the right to freedom of the individual and their responsibility to the wider society, between the right of the government to govern and its responsibility to do so only to the extent necessary for the fulfilment of its obligations.

Autonomy must be sustained by conscious acts because the apparent tendency of organisations is to centralise. This happens because where there is judgement, discretion or doubt, there is also a behavioural tendency to defer to higher authority. Once a pattern of referral is established, it becomes the norm. The model of Intelligent Organisation demands that we 'constrain autonomy no more than is necessary to sustain the cohesion of the whole' (Beckford, 2020). Temporarily setting aside any socio-political considerations about the freedom of the individual, the practical reality of contemporary organisations (whether private or public) is that the more decisions are referred to higher authorities, the slower their response time, the greater the cost of each decision, the more resources are absorbed by internal activity and the lower the overall efficiency. A side effect is that the decision maker may need a brain of extraordinary proportions to contain all the necessary knowledge and will be ridiculously busy. The risk and consequence of error increase proportionately to the referral process because the further the decision maker is from the problem or challenge, the less they can know about it and the more their decisions rely on positional authority rather than understanding. Because, and this is also inevitable, reduced local discretion leads to more decisions taken remotely, local capability falls further, a self-reinforcing, centralising cycle of referrals is established with a seemingly authoritarian culture emerging in its wake. In every instance where there is deferral to higher order decision makers, autonomy will in practical consequence be further reduced, the system for decision-making will become more centralised and more and more of the activity of the organisation will be devoted to referring matters for decision. At every level of organisation, increasing numbers of decisions will be referred to higher authority, eventually perhaps all decisions will be taken at the centre.

As I wrote this a rail infrastructure organisation, rather than fixing a relatively routine derailment and restoring services, was organising a conference about it. The lack of discretion for action will degrade both the capability of the employees and the service to the travellers. The organisation will start to fail because of the inefficiency of its operating model; it will be threatened by alternative enablers of the same outcome such as road or air travel, video conferencing, working from home. Meanwhile, people working in routine roles, constrained by the operating processes of the organisation with discretion removed, may well become disaffected, they will certainly be unfulfilled. The people, the most valuable and commonly most expensive assets of the organisation, will be used inefficiently. At the same time organisations such as the UK Core Cities Group in their green paper

'Invest, Reform, Trust' [2] argue and lobby for greater localisation proposing a substantial decentralisation and reformation of decision-making in the UK.

Beckford (2020) proposes a decision model for autonomy (Figure 2.4), a method for assessing how much autonomy is appropriate to any particular circumstance. The model suggests that individuals should do four things with their autonomy:

- apply their skills to achieve the desired outcome;
- reflect on their successes and failures and learn from them;
- communicate relevant information to those reliant upon them or upon whom they rely;
- alert higher order managers to constraints which limit their performance because only those higher order managers have legitimate power to amend the constraints.

In essence this simply asks that each individual become locally adaptive (self-regulating, self-improving), operate within the current legitimate limitations and alert those in authority to matters requiring their attention.

The model for Intelligent Organisation proposes consideration of five characteristics to assess 'how much autonomy is enough':

The Business Model: guides exploration of two dimensions, transaction volume and value. A high volume, low transaction value organisation is likely to operate with a highly process driven, automated or partly-automated process. Efficiency in such a process will require relatively low individual autonomy as the process itself will be the dominant control device. By contrast, a high transaction value, low volume organisation will have a process dominated by skills, behaviours and values. The operators, more highly skilled, will need greater autonomy to be effective in their roles. In designing an organisation, it is critical to recognise and value the skills, behaviours and values of the staff. Processes which are better delivered with an element of discretion should not be 'over-automated'. Off-setting the competing demand for efficiency through automation with sustaining sufficient discretion for staff employed is key to maintaining a viable business with a satisfied, engaged workforce. Over-automation or, worse, ineffective automation generates neither productivity nor job satisfaction.

The Process Progression: concerned with the degree of automation. Clearly the more automated the process, the less autonomy is available to the individual. Every process can be placed on a continuum from nearly complete automation to nearly zero automation and the degree of autonomy considered accordingly. Neither extreme can be reached; every process will always require some degree of human intervention (if not in the core process itself then in its preparation or completion). Similarly, every process, however apparently unique or one-off will contain elements that draw on established knowledge, practices, process routines and use of automation. Optimum job design is reached when

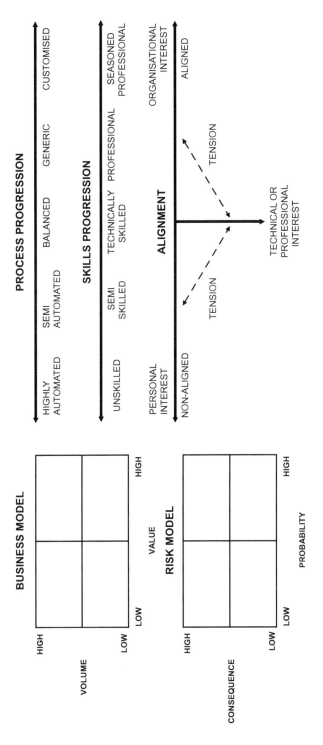

FIGURE 2.4 Decision model of autonomy

automation is balanced appropriately to the skills of the individual such that they can be most productive and engaged in the work while automation supports and enables them.

The Skills Progression: Every task requires some measure of skill for its completion. All activities can be placed along a continuum from relatively unskilled to requiring seasoned professionalism. Cross-mapping these to the process continuum, it is likely that the degree of autonomy for satisfactory completion of each process is greater for the seasoned professional conducting a low automation process than for an unskilled or low skilled worker conducting a high automation process. The demands of the process and the capability of the individual need to be aligned to deliver the appropriate process output and maintain motivation and job satisfaction. Deskilling any role at any level of organisation often leads over time to dissatisfaction through ennui and inhibits the ability to adapt and deal with changing demands and expectations.

Risk: considered along two dimensions: the probability and the consequence of adverse events. Every activity has some measure of risk which must be managed. In doing so we must be thoughtful about mitigation of either or both the likelihood (reducing the probability of an adverse event) or the consequence (acceptance that an adverse event may occur but limiting the damage that may occur). Even if possible, it is impractical (expensive, cumbersome and probably unsuccessful) to seek to mitigate all risks. Mitigation rests in some combination of process, skill and behaviour where autonomy allowed to each individual acts through process control to deliver the risk-reduced outcome. It is not intelligent to purport to manage risk by outsourcing the financial consequences of adverse events through an insurance contract; that does not address the risk itself. It is essential that individuals retain sufficient discretion, backed by training and experience, to exercise judgement in the management of risk and be able to articulate the justification for their actions.

Values Alignment: concerned with the extent to which an individuals' beliefs and values are shared or common with those of the organisation. A third dimension to this is the alignment of both with occupational or professional values and beliefs. Greatest autonomy is sustainable when the three dimensions are aligned, tension occurs when this is not the case. This reflects the requirement for a sense of identity (purpose, values and beliefs) to be shared between the leaders and the led. Legitimacy and sustainability of governance requires that there is shared identity and a legitimate process for its creation; one that exists by will and grace rather than demand and oppression. Any organisation in which duress or oppression is used to sustain leadership or management will be inefficient, will ultimately fail, torn apart by its internal contradictions.

The model is an aid to a discussion about autonomy rather than provider of a definitive outcome. The outcome must be evolutionary because the situation, the process, the people, their skills, knowledge, attitudes, the customers will continue to change. For any organisation to be viable, it is essential that autonomy is continually managed as a product of ongoing genuine discussion and participation between the parties, not a unilateral decision nor a fixed position. It is, as Fayol (interpreted by Beckford, 2017) suggested 'a question of continuously varying proportion'. This further reinforces the idea of Intelligent Organisation as continually adaptive, requiring a thoughtful and reflective rather than controlling and directive management approach; organic and systemic rather than machine like decision-making.

Resilience

The adaptiveness designed in to the Intelligent Organisation implies resilience but we need a good understanding of resilience if we are to apply the concept to a country. Applied to an individual, resilience[3] is defined as:

> the ability to adapt or rebound quickly from change, illness or bad fortune

whereas the British Standards Institute[4] describes organisational resilience as:

> the ability of an organization to anticipate, prepare for, respond and adapt to incremental change and sudden disruptions in order to survive and prosper

asserting that it is:

> a strategic imperative for an organization to prosper in today's dynamic, interconnected world. It is not a one-off exercise, but achieved over time and for the long term.

The 'ICLEI – Local Governments for Sustainability' network[5] based in Germany while not providing a definition of resilience suggests principles consistent with the ideas of this chapter (ICLEI, 2019) including the need for:

- building trust through dialogue;
- local context;
- integration;
- economic value;
- experimentation;
- curating and managing knowledge;
- anticipating change and knowledge sharing.

The United States Agency for International Development[6] defines resilience as:

the ability of people, households, communities, countries, and systems to mitigate, adapt to and recover from shocks and stresses in a manner that reduces
chronic vulnerability and facilitates inclusive growth.

The Australian (state) Governments[7] define things in relation to natural disasters
saying:

a national, coordinated and cooperative effort is required to enhance Australia's
capacity to withstand and recover from emergencies and disasters. A disaster
resilient community is one that works together to understand and manage the
risks that it confronts.

The UK Government, Civil Contingencies Secretariat, again with a focus on emergency or crisis states that:

Individual and business resilience to emergencies is about the public being
aware of risks that might impact them, or the continuity of their business,
and taking action to plan and prepare, respond and recover from these
emergencies.

The Pitt Review (2007) conducted in response to nationwide flooding in the UK
defined resilience as:

the ability of the community, services, area or infrastructure to withstand the
consequences of an incident.

and suggested that:

Resilience measures are aimed at minimising the damage when a building is
flooded, thereby facilitating the quickest possible recovery.

What is perhaps most striking about these definitions is the focus on crises, apparent
acceptance of their unavoidability and the recognition that solutions are systemic.
The emphasis on communication, information sharing, dialogue and co-operation
is excellent, but does it suggest that a stronger focus on those systemic organisational
aspects and an organisation which reflects those demands might not be better all of
the time?

Engineering is a major factor in the resilience of our national lives but is often
limited by a focus on assets. In the absence of studies of whole nation resilience, we
consider here the functional orientation of engineering and its focus on aggregating elements, which at the level of particular artefacts and assets is critical. Perhaps
it fails to express the interdependence of the whole system of assets and their value
as a whole.

Performance assessment of individual assets: Dr. Boulent Imam, University of Surrey

To understand system vulnerability we need to quantify the performance of individual assets that make up the system when affected by a hazard. When assessing the system resilience of transport infrastructure, we need to predict the performance of individual assets such as bridges, tunnels, road segments, retaining walls or slopes. We then combine them to obtain the overall system performance.

Asset performance depends on the natural and man-made hazards that affect the asset over its lifetime as well as the exposure of the asset to such hazards. Natural hazards include principally floods caused by heavy rain, landslides, earthquakes, storms wind and extreme temperatures. Man-made hazards include accidental actions such as collisions on a bridge or a retaining wall, a ship impact on a bridge pier or a bomb attack. Asset performance is also dependent on the long-term degradation and ageing of the asset due to its exposure to long-term environmental effects or fatigue due to cyclic loading from traffic. While metallic bridges deteriorate over time due to the effects of atmospheric corrosion, reinforced concrete assets deteriorate due to the effects of carbonation or chloride-induced corrosion. For risk assessment, it is important to capture both the effects of long-term degradation and one-off hazards on an asset's performance within the same framework because the starting condition is important to asset performance under load.

Asset performance can be measured in terms of functionality or the level of service provided including availability and reliability. Availability can be defined as the percentage of time that an asset is capable of functioning and is largely a function of the frequency and duration of downtime. Reliability is the ability of an asset to perform its required function(s) under stated conditions for a specified period of time; often expressed as a probability of failure.

Consequences of asset failure

An appropriate assessment of asset failure risk requires estimation of the consequences of failure, which play an essential role in both qualitative and quantitative risk-based design and assessment.

Direct or indirect consequences of failure are a good indicator of the importance of a bridge structure, given its form, function and location within a transport network. They can range from casualties and injuries to structural damage, reduction in network functionality and may also extend into environmental as well as societal impact. Table 2.1 shows that, in general, consequences resulting from bridge failures may be divided into four main categories: human, economic, environmental and social. Each of these main four categories can be

TABLE 2.1 Consequences of bridge failure

Consequence categories	Examples
Human	Fatalities
	Injuries
	Psychological damage
Economic	Replacement/repair costs
	Loss of functionality/downtime
	Traffic delay/re-routing costs
	Traffic management costs
	Clean-up costs
	Rescue costs
	Regional economic effects
	Loss of production/business
	Investigations/compensations
	Infrastructure inter-dependency costs
Environmental	CO_2 emissions
	Energy use
	Pollutant releases
	Environmental clean-up/reversibility
Social	Loss of reputation
	Erosion of public confidence
	Undue changes in professional practice

further sub-divided into a number of more specific areas, so that itemisation and appropriate modelling, where possible, may be undertaken.

Direct consequences are considered to result from damage to individual components. Indirect consequences, triggered by the former, are associated with reduction in, or loss of, system functionality and can be linked to the level of robustness. The differentiation between direct and indirect consequences is somewhat subjective depending on the system boundaries considered in the analysis as well as on the time frame employed.

A modelling framework for bridge failure consequences should account for their type, the relevant time frame, as well as the system boundaries surrounding the structure. The time frame considered plays an important role in consequence modelling; consequences will be different when considering only a short-term post-event time frame or a long-term period extending well after the failure event. The actual duration in considering long-term periods is also expected to affect the magnitude of estimated consequences. For example, a bridge failure may result during the immediate and mid-term aftermath, in loss of business revenue and high traffic delay costs but over longer periods these might change as new regional equilibria are reached. Lastly, consequence estimation is affected by the definition of the system boundaries; for example, the system may be defined as solely the structural system of the bridge (structural domain) or it may be extended into the transportation network that the bridge is within (spatial domain). The extent of the spatial domain is also an important factor, depending on whether a single route (with diversions) or a more widely encompassing spatial network is considered. Here, the level of redundancy of the transportation network in redistributing traffic flows following the bridge collapse plays an important role. Further layers can be added to the above systems by addressing wider societal consequences such as business losses, environmental impact, etc.

The consequences of failure vary significantly depending on a range of factors related to the hazard itself, the structure and its utilisation and the surrounding environment. The source and nature of the hazard leading to the bridge collapse will considerably affect the consequences although essentially the greater the magnitude and duration of a hazard, the greater the consequences.

Bridge location is a major factor influencing the magnitude of failure consequences. The type of road or rail route served by the bridge influences the traffic intensity and, hence, the number of people exposed to any given hazard, as well as the traffic delay costs. Moreover, the availability of emergency services and accessibility to treatment for injuries will most likely be best in urban areas reducing human costs. Finally, the cost of restoration of the bridge structure may be higher in rural areas due to increased labour, materials and transportation costs although access might be easier and inter-dependency issues reduced compared to urban areas.

Written from a distinctly civil engineering perspective, this study nonetheless highlights a number of key features of systems that we need to keep in mind. Those features are the idea of interdependence, the dynamic relationships in modelling between time, location, utilisation, restoration and both economic and social consequences and the subjectivity of choices made about boundaries. These call on the professional to make informed judgements about any particular situation and to understand the need for resilience in multiple dimensions.

The Intelligent Organisation is systemic and designed to be inherently resilient. Reflecting the idea of Ashby's (1956) Ultrastable Homeostat and linking to the cybernetic notion of feedforward (anticipatory and ideative) control, it seeks to evade or pre-empt a crisis rather than mitigate its harm, reduce impact and ensure rapid recovery. If the system does not fail, it does not need to recover, the Black Swan (Taleb, 2010) as Beckford[8] suggests does not materialise. Perhaps robustness needs to be understood as much as resilience with fragility designed out. Pre-emption and evasion of crisis demands that any organisation have capacity and capability in its processes, speed of response, communication channels and its temporal, corporeal and ethereal resources that it is able to deal even with abnormal perturbations. It cannot do that when organised around a centralised, functionally oriented structure with low local autonomy.

Reformation or revolution

Considering the observed state as outlined in the first chapter with the design and expectations of the Intelligent Organisation, it becomes clear that there is a gap to be closed.

Over specialisation has seen that Parkinson's Law (1986) that 'work expands so as to fill the time available for its completion' has fully taken effect. The pathological autopoiesis evident in bureaucratically designed and operated public organisations drives a situation where more and more of the allocated resources are absorbed in sustaining the organisation, with a decreasing proportion devoted to the achievement of the desired outcome. Sight of that desired outcome has been lost, diverted or converted to other ends, the original problem having been solved, resolved or dissolved. Meanwhile challenges change and evolve, but the institutions established to address them lack the capacity to adapt to the emerging requirements remaining 'trapped in an insanity of tradition' (Beckford, 2020).

Attempts are being made on a continuing basis to alter this situation, to change, transform, redesign organisations, but they cannot succeed while the solution is rooted in the same thinking that caused the problem. A whole new approach is required, one which looks at the outcomes desired by the customers, which focuses on their achievement and allows higher order organisations and institutions to emerge from local engagement rather than be devolved from the centre. There is a need for both local and national organisations and the tension between them to be managed and this can only be done when the individual is both resilient and engaged through a citizen-focussed, process-driven and outcome-oriented organisation. If a nation is to be intelligent, its organisation and governance must be reformed. This means considering the role, competencies and powers of all governmental activities whether national, state, city and metropolitan or town. Within each their structure and organisation must be revisited and rendered appropriate to our current and future needs. In the UK, while the Blair government's devolution of powers to the Scottish parliament and the Welsh and Northern Ireland Assemblies is subject to continuing battles over rights and obligations and reform of the House of Lords is widely regarded as incomplete, Regional and City Mayors are emerging. Each of these political arms of government seeks its legitimate role, while their duties and obligations to some extent overlap and it is in the nature of politicians to seek to extend their reach. Each of these elements of the State has a set of officers and creates a set of local civil services intended to execute the policies of the politicians. The boundaries are unclear, the benefits even more so, the costs ever increasing.

Summary

This chapter proposes that we adopt cybernetic principles to redesign our nation backwards from the citizen so that it can fulfil the agreed purposes through a legitimate government. To do this, values, behaviours, systems and processes must be fully integrated and decentralised as far as is practicable with promotion and enhancement of local citizen autonomy. The fundamental building block for that is the resilient citizen, the meaning of which is the next topic for consideration.

Key points

The Intelligent Organisation developed from cybernetic principles provides a design for an Intelligent Nation;

The principles of a cybernetic organisation are the systems principle, the black box principle, the principle of self-regulation, and the law of requisite variety;

It is designed to continuously resolve three challenges simultaneously: managing the present, creating the future, and nurturing identity;

An Intelligent Nation is purposeful, and it has direction and intent;

Legitimacy of governance depends on consent;

An integrated organisation is made of four elements;
– Value-Generating Processes
– Value-Enabling Processes
– A Trialogue (a synthesis of gubernatorial discussions)
– An integrating information system dealing with both qualitative and quantitative information.

Customer Outcomes are the basis of design;

Autonomy must be designed in and sustained;

Resilience of the individual is crucial to viability, and resilience of the nation emerges from that.

References

Ashby, W.R., (1956) *An Introduction to Cybernetics*, Chapman & Hall, London

Avis, P.D.L., (2008) *The Identity of Anglicanism: Essentials of Anglican Ecclesiology*, Bloomsbury T&T Clark, London

Beckford, J., (1993) *The Viable System Model: A More Adequate Tool for Practising Management*, PhD Thesis, University of Hull

Beckford, J., (2017) *Quality, A Critical Introduction,* 4th edition, Routledge, London

Beckford, J., (2020) *The Intelligent Organisation: Driving Systemic Change with Information*, 2nd edition, Routledge, London

Beer, S., (1974) *Designing Freedom*, Wiley, Chichester

Beer, S., (1979) *The Heart of Enterprise*, Wiley, Chichester

Beer, S., (1981) *Brain of the Firm*, Wiley, Chichester

Beer, S., (1985) *Diagnosing the System for Organisations*, Wiley, Chichester

Cabinet Office Pitt, M., (2007) *Pitt Review: Learning Lessons from the 2007 Floods*, HM Government, Crown Copyright

Clemson, B., (1984) *Cybernetics: A New Management Tool*, Abacus Press, Kent, UK

Curtice, J., Clery, E., Perry, J., Phillips M. & Rahim, N., (eds.) (2019), *British Social Attitudes: The 36th Report*, London: The National Centre for Social Research

Davie, G., (2016) "Establishment" in *The Oxford Handbook of Anglican Studies*, pp. 287–300, Chapman, M., Clarke, S., Percy, M., (eds.), Oxford University Press, Oxford

Deming, W.E., (1986) *Out of the Crisis*, The Press Syndicate, Cambridge, UK

Dudley, P., (1998) "Food for trees: Man's place in the tapestry of life on earth," *Kybernetes*, Vol. 27 No. 2, pp. 165–169

Dudley, P., (2000) *Quality Management or Management Quality? An adaptive model of organisation as the basis of organisational learning and quality provision.* PhD Thesis, The University of Hull

Gödel, K (1929) *Über die Vollständigkeit des Logikkalküls*. Doctoral dissertation. University of Vienna

Hall, J.A., (1998) *The State of the Nation*, Cambridge University Press, Cambridge

Hart, D.B., (2009) *Atheistic Delusions: The Christian Revolution and Its Fashionable Enemies*, Yale University Press, New Haven and London

Hobsbawm, E.J., (1990) *Nations and Nationalism since 1780*, Cambridge University Press, Cambridge

ICLEI, (2019) *Thriving Cities: The Evolution of Urban Resilience*, Bonn, Germany

MacCulloch, D., (2009) *A History of Christianity*, Allen Lane, London

O'Toole, F., (2018) *Heroic Failure: Brexit and the Politics of Pain*, Head of Zeus, London

Parkinson, C.N., (1986) *Parkinson's Law or The Pursuit of Progress*, Penguin, London

Plato, (390 BC approx.), *Alcibiades*

Ryrie, A., (2016) "The Reformation in Anglicanism" in *The Oxford Handbook of Anglican Studies*, pp. 34–45, Chapman, M., Clarke, S., Percy, M., (eds.), Oxford University Press, Oxford

Smith, A.D., (1991) *National Identity*, Penguin, London

Taleb, N., (2010) *The Black Swan*, Penguin, London

Taylor, C., (2007) *A Secular Age*, The Belknap Press of Harvard University Press, Cambridge, MA

United Nations Development Programme, (2019), *Human Development Report*, New York, NY 10017 USA

Ulrich, W., (1983) *Critical Heuristics of Social Planning*, Haupt, Berne

Yan, S., (2019) *The Telegraph Magazine*, Spy pp. 31–35, Telegraph Media Group, London

Notes

1. https://humanprogress.org/article.php?p=256 10/02/2020
2. https://www.corecities.com/publications/invest-reform-trust-core-cities-green-paper-stronger-fairer-britain 06/02/2020
3. https://psychologydictionary.org/resilience/ 05/02/2020
4. https://www.bsigroup.com/en-GB/our-services/Organizational-Resilience/ 05/02/2020
5. https://iclei.org/en/About_ICLEI_2.html 05/02/2020
6. https://www.usaid.gov/resilience 05/02/2020
7. https://www.homeaffairs.gov.au/emergency/files/national-strategy-disaster-resilience.pdf 05/02/2020
8. https://beckfordconsulting.com/misc/the-paradoxical-black-swan-in-the-overgrowth/

3
SUSTAINABLE AND RESILIENT CITIZEN

Introduction

An Intelligent Nation needs intelligent citizens: resilient people from whose actions and interactions that nation emerges. The citizens are the nation; they populate the value-generating and value-enabling processes, bringing them to life. Citizens collectively create the culture, values and beliefs, and the state (the services and infrastructure provided by and through local and national government) is an emergent property of their interactions, the realisation of their demands and the product of the things they will accept and those that they won't, governed through effective democratic processes.

It is essential to think about an idealised individual as an Intelligent Organisation (Beckford, 2020). The individual is the heart of a nation, its ultimate source of current and future value (economic, social and environmental) and as such there is no point in an aspiration to mediocrity. The synthesis of the physiological and psychological dimensions of the idealised individual with a range of knowledge, attributes and skills enables the emergence of a resilient citizen, society and nation, rooted in a shared sense of belonging. The core assumption is acceptance and action on the belief that every individual, whether engaged in value-enabling or value-generating activity, has equal potential and every individual must receive equal opportunity, while acknowledging that some people will always require support while all people will sometimes need it. The behavioural role and responsibility of the powerful, influential and privileged in an Intelligent Nation is to support and enable others, to create, generate and stimulate opportunities for others whose immediate position is less advantageous. Regardless of starting position, all people must have the opportunity to fulfil their potential, to self-realise (Maslow, 1970) or self-actualise, to be their best selves.

Considering the current state of affairs, there is much that we must change to make that possible. There is gross disbalance between the power of the individual and the state and to balance this we must both amplify the capability of the individual and attenuate the variety of the state. The primacy of the individual must be asserted, and they, not the state, must be structurally recognised as the source of power and wealth. There is a risk, maybe a deliberate policy by some, to use language as a boundary, a device for exclusion. Language and concepts must be adopted that are inclusive rather than exclusive, that actively seek to embrace others and that recognise the potential for language as an instrument of power which can be used and abused. Space for reflection, for discussion and challenge and the development of shared meaning must be created. Ultimately, citizens must be angry and dissatisfied with how things are and apply their energy and power to change them and to support others. While structurally we must recognise the contribution that each person makes, we must listen to the views of others and behave reasonably to them even if and when, perhaps especially if and when, we disagree with them.

Those with power and influence must not reserve it for themselves by simply managing the present but use the understanding of Intelligent Organisation to create opportunities for creating the future, for the ideas and insights of others to be shared and opened to the possibility of realisation; no one has a monopoly on such things. An earlier blog explains.

Opening doors: Dr. John Beckford

While thinking about this post I enjoyed a conversation with my adult sons about the nature and use of organisational power. The conversation considered markets and their failures, the impact of dominant actors in those markets and the often-distorting effects of regulation. Consideration of natural world eco-systems followed, contemplating how, in the main (and if not unduly distorted by the actions of mankind) they often reach a state of dynamic equilibrium over time. This brought to mind an earlier paper (Beckford, 1994) on the tendency of capital (including intellectual capital) to centralise and inhibit innovation.

This gave rise to some speculation:

Is higher education distorted by its performance regime?
What is the responsibility of the academic in enabling innovation?

While a market failure may correct itself, a small number of dominant actors sustained in their position by regulation or intervention because they are 'too big to fail' are likely to consume all the resources. The market will fail!

This thinking was sharpened, partly by the pressing submission deadline, partly from a visit to Robben Island where both Nelson Mandela and Jacob Zuma were held as political prisoners. Prisoners of a system in which the 'market had failed' – political 'regulation' acted to sustain the societal status quo.

It was humbling to reflect on the strength of mind and spirit required of Mandela, in such deliberately dispiriting circumstances, to write and preserve 'The Long Walk to Freedom', (Mandela, 1995, Little Brown & Co.) The guide, an ex-political prisoner himself, explained that education for prisoners was a privilege not a right and how, circumventing the rules, the prisoners would quietly self-organise into study groups so that those who already had education and knowledge could share it with their fellows, where Mandela is reported to have said 'Let this be our university'.

I wonder if the emphasis was on 'this' or 'our' – or both? Try reading it aloud a couple of times – it makes a big difference!

In an eco-system, the big beasts eat until they are sated – and then stop. In human systems, it seems that the big beasts sometimes don't know when they are full and continue to pursue food (power and wealth) seemingly for its own sake and not for some higher purpose. Once in a dominant position they seek to optimise the market in their own favour, working to establish a regulatory environment which sustains them despite their failings. They become 'too big to fail'.

This led me to consider use of power and for me, it must rest with the individual not the institution. Institutional behaviour is perhaps an aggregation of the behaviour of all the human actors within it.

What has that got to do with Information Science (I would probably ask if I was assessing this piece of work!). What's the point?

The task of the academic, whether researcher, teacher or both is to discern new ways of understanding the world and have impact in that world. That is, we are expected to share insights and new knowledge in a form that enables the insight and wisdom of others.

In the technology-driven, big data, cloud computing world, the Information Scientist has a particularly important role. We have an obligation to comprehend, design, interpret and translate this world, to open it to the examination and testing not of our peers (that we can take for granted) but of all the individuals whose lives are affected by and affect technology – as well as those who effect it.

The demands of the 'system' – the REF, acquisition of research grants and pursuit of promotion – are such that self-interest is best served by the imprisoning of information while the responsibility of the Information Scientist (and perhaps all academics) is to liberate it. Thereby each individual can be encouraged and enabled to acquire information, knowledge, perhaps wisdom and empower her or himself. Ultimately each can determine rightness in their own terms and their own appreciation of the world they want to have. Then they can all argue about it! They can, normally attributed to Ghandi, 'be the change they want to see in the world'.

Surely, the obligation of the powerful is to discern, create or enable opportunities for those less powerful than themselves, to open the doors – with suitable force if necessary – to 'give a break' to others even if, or perhaps especially when, it disrupts the established hegemony.

We, the powerful, must allow others to develop and shape their own future – even if it is not the one we would choose for them (or impose on them!) We must stimulate opportunities for them to be the person they are able to be not a pale imitation of the established experts or indeed to be the 'gaolers of their own future' Nobbs (2009)

Is success then about how clever I enable you to be, rather than how clever I am? How many doors have YOU kicked open for others?

It is not sufficient simply to declare equality of opportunity; if we are to build a resilient, Intelligent Nation, those who hold power must deliberately create opportunities for those currently without, failure to do so will undermine the nation. A key element in viability rests in maximising the autonomy of the individual so that effective responses to challenges can be made as close to source as possible.

Human beings learn by reducing error, by acknowledging the dissonance between how we perceive things and how we would like them to be, reasoning about causes and acting to close the gap. To do this, there must an aspiration to a desired future state (the other side of Plato's harbour), as well as comprehension of the current state. The gap is the basis of individual and state action. A fully inclusive society is a core requirement for an Intelligent Nation, not only because that is fair and just for the individual but also because it delivers the greatest potential benefit to all its members. However, we must address some important questions:

How do we (re)design public services to enable and support equality of opportunity for all?

How do we ensure that differences of ethnicity, nationality, sexuality, religion, faith, physical and mental ability or disability, socio-economic background do not artificially inhibit individual prospects or achievement?

How do we evaluate and understand whether each individual is able to obtain and utilise the opportunity to become their best self?

How do we manage our democracy to ensure that it is equitable, vital and viable?

In a country conceived as an Intelligent Nation, it is the responsibility of all to use power and influence for the benefit of the whole. To achieve that, to create the future, requires investment in the development of each person to build their confidence and the capability to push themselves forward, to be courageous, to believe in themselves, be proud of who they are and exploit opportunities generated. Of particular concern is to ensure that opportunities are made available to those most disadvantaged by current arrangements, including those unconventionally qualified, from unusual routes and to address those who are capable of being in employment, training or education but, for whatever reason, are not.

If the Intelligent Nation is to be realised, then politicians, whether local, regional or national, must be reminded that they are elected to pursue the promises (a product of their espoused beliefs and values) they make to the electorate. Citizens invite politicians to exercise power on their behalf; politicians are the servants of the people at whose behest they continue in office. Each aspect of what is required for an individual to enable themselves as an Intelligent Organisation must be considered. In thinking about resilience, we will need to consider physical and mental capabilities as well as health, education, skills, training, family or other social support, finance, employment and housing. We will need to ensure that embracing inclusiveness, diversity and equality complements the equality of opportunity demanded. If everyone is to have equal opportunity to be the best that they can be, there are profound implications for the ways we sustain democracy and recognise and incorporate interdependency in the design and delivery of both public services and infrastructure because, as is clear to any observer, that is far from the case at present.

The individual as Intelligent Organisation

The Intelligent Organisation (Beckford, 2020) offered here is a way of helping each of us to order and structure our thinking about ourselves. It is most usefully thought of as a way of teasing apart some of the numerous strands of our existence rather than as a technocratic or structural 'solution'. Remember, cybernetics is about ways of behaving and ways of behaving rely on ways of thinking, so use this to help that thinking.

Each of us must generate and enable value for ourselves, to be self-organising in delivery of outputs and achievement of desired outcomes. We must manage our resources (including information) and do so in the context of the nested sets of relationships of family, work, friends and the state that enable or inhibit our lives. We must do the same three things as any other organisation in order to thrive; we must manage our present, create our future and resolve the tension between the two by understanding and nurturing our identity and fulfilling our purpose (see Figure 3.1). This requires that we develop a clear sense of 'self', of who we are, our place in the world and how the various roles we play in life enable self-fulfilment. Perhaps we are fulfilled when we are being our best self?

Managing the present, the regulation of our value-generating activities, describes the need to control our current activities and balance the allocation of our resources (time, energy, money) across them. It acts to maintain our stability in relation to our

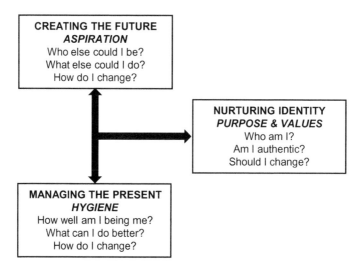

FIGURE 3.1 Personal trialogue: Elements of self

current roles and commitments, doing what we do now but aiming to improve with each iteration. Each of us plays a number of roles in our lives. I am contemporaneously husband, father, consultant, author, researcher and volunteer; I never stop being all of them although the focus of my effort at any moment will be on one. Each of those roles represents one aspect of my total existence, one way in which I seek to generate valuable outcomes for others and for myself. We each play multiple roles, some similar to mine, some different, mother, daughter, son, worker, leader, scientist, engineer, all of these words describe things we do, ways in which we seek to exchange value with the world.

Value itself is multi-faceted; it is not simply transactional, considering contracts and monetary exchange (which benefit our financial position), but about authentic, meaningful relationships with people and organisations which affect our sense of well-being, are not injurious to our health or damaging to our family or to others and which support our personal sustainability. The financial system in which we operate demands that we generate enough revenue over time to meet our expenditure, so finance is important, but as has been shown in various studies on motivation[1] beyond a certain level (varying with each individual and their circumstances), it does not stimulate us to greater effort, whereas both praise and opportunity do.

Creating the future, the regulation of our value-enabling activities, is concerned with exploring the challenges and opportunities in our surrounding environments as well as the changes in ourselves (aspirations, needs, skills, behaviours). It seeks to resolve or dissolve threats and discover alternative ways of sustaining our existence, generating actions which both modify our environment and stimulate alteration to ourselves. It acts to drive change by highlighting alternative roles that we could play or alternative ways of playing the same role, of stimulating new knowledge, different skills, attributes and behaviours through which our future selves may be realised. These future selves can of course be both threat and opportunity driven with our world view often influencing how information is received; what presents as a threat may, differently interpreted, be turned to our advantage.

The Intelligent Organisation is inherently adaptive whereas there is a widely held belief in the theory and practise of organisational change that creating the future, that is, actively seeking change, is resisted. Many authors consider that formal action is required to overcome the resistance and enable change to take place. Lewin (1947) proposed that we must 'unfreeze, change, refreeze', while Hammer and Champy (1993) pursued wholesale re-engineering and more recently, Seddon (2008) focuses primarily on public sector reform. There is a whole industry of change practitioners from individuals and corporate entities and coaches to therapists and 'change practices' from both large- and small-consultancy organisations built on treating change as the exception. Instead of assuming that change is abnormal, the Intelligent Organisation sees it as an evolutionary necessity, an adaptation to changing circumstances and conceives its management differently. Keynes is reputed to have said that 'When the facts change, I change my mind' or words to that effect. Being diligent in exploring our possible futures and our circumstances, if the information we are receiving changes, then it is irrational not to adapt accordingly. Change is not a discrete and occasional event, but a continuing stream of ideations and responses to opportunities and threats in our environment. We must overturn the prevailing assumptions about continuity, accept that change is continual and that it either needs to be achieved at the same rate and scale as the arrival of perturbations or we need sufficient resilience to absorb and attenuate the shocks, or both.

The real challenge, where resistance becomes apparent, is when possible futures clash with the perceived present. Current roles, skills and activities are dominant; they consume time, control resources, reaffirm current position and they define the 'future we are currently in' (Ackoff, 1981). Diverting resources and effort away from the present assumes that there are spare resources to divert. If spare resources (savings) are low, resilience will also be low. The present self has to be persuaded to cede resources (time, energy, money) to the future self and if those are inadequate something must give. The future is perceived to contain new or unmitigated risks and unknowns, whereas the present contains the comforting illusion of certainty. Being comfortable with continuity, with dissonance unarticulated, it is always easier in the short term to manage the present. However, maintaining the status quo is not always feasible, appropriate or desirable. Standing still is not an option when the environment of family, work, technology, politics and so on are dynamic; they change regardless of the individual. Handy (1990) talks of the risk of discontinuous change saying that a frog placed in cold water which is then heated will be so comfortable with the steadily continuing change in temperature, that it will boil to death before it realises it is in danger. We know that change is happening; we tolerate and accept it until perhaps, quite suddenly, the circumstances no longer sustain us. Taleb (2010) suggests that we cannot always know or predict when an unforeseeable, maybe unsurvivable, change will occur; sometimes that can only be seen in retrospect.

Tensions exist between our present and future selves, between the person we perceive ourselves to be (represented by our roles, behaviours, skills, knowledge and relationships) and the person we believe we need to be in the future with whatever changes may be required. The present restrains us; the future beckons us with opportunity but promises hard work, risk and uncertainty.

Nurturing identity

We resolve the tension by nurturing our sense of identity, by knowing who we are and what matters to us. Nurturing identity, the third element of the trialogue, is the set of actions we take in order to maintain our sense of self by appreciating our purpose and intent and the set of values that underpin them. These values help us to identify what is important to us, what matters and, most importantly, why.

These aspects are all generally much easier to describe and deal with in relation to an organisation than they are to individuals, partly because when externalised, they can be described in abstract terms, partly because we often pay lip-service to them. Organisational values are often distanced from the individual, espoused but not lived. Obliged to confront them at the personal level, they are much harder, often because we have not given them much thought, but we do what we do because we are who we are; our actions are the observable practise of our values. Knowing who we are, deciding what is really important to us, is key to our sense of satisfaction and our contentment as well as enabling us to make choices between the present and the possible futures. Articulating those choices and their rationale simplifies decisions and those who know our values will be able to make useful assertions about our likely choices.

Our values are an expression of our ethics, morality, honesty, integrity and religious belief or its absence. They are informed by our upbringing, our individual lived experience, our exposure to differing cultures and beliefs and fundamental, technical and professional education. Most importantly, they are affected by how we have reflected on our accumulated knowledge and experience, adapted to it and reflected on the lived experience of others. All of that, taken together, informs the hopes and ambitions, the sense of purpose which will vary widely from those who want to change the world to those content with how things are, those who demand difference and those comfortable with their particular status quo. Whatever the position of any one person, it provides a sense of purpose and identity to inform decisions. There can be no 'right answer', simply the authentic decisions of thoughtful individuals.

Managing the Present, Creating the Future and Nurturing Identity come together in the personal trialogue (Figure 3.1) a complex, dynamic, evolving set of choices about who we wish to be. Considering this, a behavioural challenge rooted in our individual responses which becomes replicated in the organisations we create, must be confronted. Perhaps evolutionarily useful, many people focus on the immediate operational challenge, the short-term fix, and shy away from longer-term considerations. Many appear more comfortable with the apparent certainty of resolving an immediately presenting threat or opportunity than with more nebulous longer-term possibilities with all the necessarily unknowns and potential risks that entails. They seek the intrinsic satisfaction of 'solution' and, in many circumstances, are rewarded extrinsically as well. The system in which they perform rewards them with additional pay, praise, promotion, job security for being operationally effective. This phenomenon is well articulated in the work of Kahnemann (2011) and Peters (2012) with the consideration of our emotional and rational responses to stimuli of various sorts. Mischel (2014), by contrast, describes the Marshmallow Test, an experiment on young children, which promises one marshmallow immediately or two a little later if the child can defer the pleasure of the marshmallow for a short period. Mischel goes on to show that those children who can defer pleasure are more likely to 'succeed' (education, career, etc.) in life as they grow, suggesting that thinking about future reward is a critical determinant of long-term success.

The challenge for all of us is to learn to offset the immediate gratification of the short-term, perhaps temporary, answer against the sustained long-term dissolution of a problem. The ability to do so may be critical to our personal resilience.

Personal resilience

A resilient citizen will be protected from the state and empowered to deal with its might and complexity both by their own capability and by the system of legislation and governance that they will co-create with fellow citizens. Such a citizen is an Intelligent Organisation, resilient and robust with fragility designed out. Lacy[2] suggests five characteristics of resilience:

> Perspective: gaining distance, focusing on things which can be changed, accepting what cannot;
> Emotional Intelligence: aware of and accepting of our own emotions and those of others, altruistic in approach;
> Purpose, Values, Strengths: alignment of what we do with what we value and believe in;
> Connections: maintaining and drawing on a network, gaining strength from it;
> Managing Physical Energy: maintaining physical well-being through diet, exercise, relaxation, however much pressure is exerted.

Although this model was developed around leadership, individuals are at least the leaders in their own lives, and the requirements are consistent with characteristics already considered for the Intelligent Organisation. A resilient individual, being their best self and living their best life at any given time, will need access to housing, healthcare, money, education, employment and a network of support whether that be family, friends, colleagues or other contacts. Each will need the skills and behaviours necessary to cope with a difficult and demanding world and the insight and wisdom to not become ensnared by ill-informed decisions. Everyone must have access to educational provision that allows them to develop their own perspective and enable meaningful, fully informed, choices. Creating these circumstances is a responsibility for those who hold power to create and it is not always lived up to. As the following example on the current cost and benefit of university education in the UK shows, we must be beware of setting traps which create the illusion of increasing opportunity while potentially reducing it; if we are not fully informed, our freedom is delusory.

Another fine mess: Dr. John Beckford[3]

Settling down to write a blog for the School [of Business and Economics, Loughborough University], I stumbled across this letter to a Vice-Chancellor and thought I would share it with you instead. I have only tidied it up a bit and remembered the title from Laurel and Hardy!

Dear Vice-Chancellor,

I am being pressed by my parents and school to complete my UCAS form and personal statement and get on with my university applications. I am a diligent student so I have done the background things, I have looked at the university brochures, I have read in the Times Higher about government education policy and the various challenges facing Universities. I saw in the paper (Telegraph I think) a couple of weeks ago that the average debt of a graduating student is £87,000, meanwhile I also read Beckford's blog http://intelligentorganisation.com/uncategorised/university-challenged/[4] which set out the basic cost-benefit argument.

My Dad, meanwhile bangs on about what a wonderful opportunity university provides. Back in the day, the first from his family to go to university (red-brick), he got a grant – he was practically paid for being at university and worked on building sites in the summer for extra cash. Once he is a couple of beers in to the conversation, life seems to have revolved around sunshine, lying on the grass, smoking some of it, quoting Bill and Ben esp. Little Weed, Kafka, Chomsky, Wittgenstein and Confucius and pondering the meaning of eclectic while listening to Pink Floyd.

My Mum on the other hand worries about me getting into debt and, to be frank, living where we do, £87,000 would be enough to buy a small house – but when I want to do that, I will already have that amount hanging over me for 30 years! Mum also worries about what she calls the 'laddish' culture at university, she is concerned that I should not be in a place where sexual activity is expected or coerced.

I find it a bit strange that at nearly 18 I can have sex (provided it is not with someone under 16 or coerced by an adult with responsibility for me), smoke a cigarette, drink alcohol with a meal and if caught in possession of illegal drugs likely only get cautioned and drive a car – though not all at the same time. I can't though vote in elections or in the referendum on Europe the outcome of which will dictate a large part of my future.

I can, though, commit to getting into debt.

I understand also that as part of Europe I can apply to attend a university in another country. I heard of one boy who is applying to a place in Poland where the course is taught in English and he will pay no fees. Although we can't learn Polish at my school, no fees and a much lower cost of living is quite appealing.

I already have an AS in Mathematics and am taking English, History and French through to A Level. My Dad says it is important that, if I go, I study something I am interested in. I want to study archaeology and maybe become an archaeologist. My Mum argues with him that there is no point in getting into debt studying a subject she describes as 'about as much use as a chocolate teapot when it comes to making a living'. My Dad counters her with an argument that it doesn't matter what I study, the point of going to university is to learn something about a particular subject and in doing so to learn how to research, to critically review, to construct and defend my own arguments about the subject but most of all to grow up and learn to take responsibility for myself and my life. He says once I have demonstrated graduate ability loads of employers will be open to me – but it seems to me from what I read and hear that more and more employers want graduates who are 'work-ready', which implies I must acquire skills relevant to the job rather than the subject knowledge I need to graduate. That baffles me too: is university about learning things or work skills?

Trouble is, as I see it, that I first have to take the decision I understand least; before I have learned to construct and defend my own arguments and take responsibility, I have to take the decision about borrowing money. And if it doesn't work out, then I am stuck with it. If I buy something from a shop and it doesn't work, then I am entitled to a refund; yet if I pay to go to University and I don't benefit from it as I expect, then it is, apparently, my fault, the university has no liability – but it is the university that provides the product or service?

So, this is my dilemma, Vice-Chancellor. I don't know what to do and thought that, perhaps, as you are in charge of a university you might be able to advise me?

Eve Ryman

What could I, your blogger, possibly add?

How can we develop intelligent, resilient individuals if, before they reach the age of majority, we are seducing them into life-defining decisions, the implications of which they have not been educated to comprehend? How can we develop intelligent, resilient individuals if we preside over a system which has the effect of excluding the aspirational because of their parents' means?

Emotional intelligence (Maddocks, 2014) is concerned with 'an individual's effectiveness and performance' rather than their inherent predispositions or behaviours arguing that it can be changed and developed, whereas inherent traits are largely fixed. Hills (2016), defining resilience as the capability to recover from stress or adversity, argues that emotionally intelligent people are also emotionally resilient; they are able to manage and recover from problems and challenges, what has been called here robustness. Active encouragement will enable all people, especially perhaps the disadvantaged and less traditional, non-conventional, nervous or fragile, to grasp opportunity. In succeeding they can build robustness; they can become anti-fragile. To achieve this, a social environment is needed in which all people can be fully informed, assisted where necessary, so that they are able to make their own decisions. We must ensure everyone has the confidence to try and appropriately support if they do not at first succeed. A key part of that will rest in a set of emotionally supportive relationships which, without being patronising or restrictive, assist individuals in comprehending the consequences of their decisions and those of others. Assisting everyone to develop strong emotional resilience will also assist them in dealing with matters of material welfare.

In thinking of ourselves as intelligent organisations, all this fits well with the notion of adaptation, of changing as well as learning. Perspective lets us comprehend a situation; emotional intelligence and resilience lets us deal with the personal consequences, our inherent ability for adaptation based on use of information provides the mechanism while our sense of purpose and values aligns our responses with our beliefs.

Taking the last elements of Lacy's model out of order, we can consider the material aspect of resilience. Here Lacy refers to physical well-being, exercise and relaxation as contributory elements of personal resilience. However, there are a range of other aspects, what Herzberg et al. (1959) might have called 'hygiene factors', the absence of which are limiting to personal resilience and damaging to aspiration and achievement of purpose. These factors are, at least, housing, education, employment, healthcare, energy, money. While their presence will not necessarily motivate the individual, their absence will both undermine the ability to compete on equal terms and substantially detract from resilience by increasing the fragility of their existence. Murray (2019) describes how despite increasing urbanisation 'We definitely know more about good habitats for mountain gorillas, Siberian tigers or panda bears than we do about a good urban habitat for Homo Sapiens'. McArthur and Paul,[5] considering the housing situation in New Zealand, have shown how 'the housing affordability crisis hits young people – particularly Māori and low-income groups – the hardest', commenting that established policies cater mainly to the interests of existing property owners confirming the critique raised by Beckford (1994). They go on to note that the situation could change if only young people would vote. Similar differences will be found in other areas of life. The NHS in the UK is often accused of operating a 'postcode lottery' with Pym[6] in 2017, saying there are 'diverging trends in England for a range of procedures, including colonoscopy and hip operations'. In the USA Startz (2010) suggests a similar uneven distribution, this time of education: 'Some of our schools are first rate; others are disastrous. On average, our schools aren't terrible – they're mediocre. C+ quality schools portend a C+ quality future'. It seems that inequality of distribution is embedded deeply in the way public services are organised, detracting from the material resilience and capability of individuals and acting to amplify disadvantage, not by intent but as the emergent outcome of established policy and behaviour.

Unsurprisingly, the most disadvantaged financially are often, though not exclusively, the most disadvantaged in other aspects such as education, healthcare, housing and employment. These disadvantages interact, reinforcing each other and it is hard to break free from these aspects of relative deprivation. Hills (2015) provocatively argues that, over a lifetime in the UK, each of us contributes to and draws upon public services and benefits and that in doing so the scales balance suggesting that whether wealthy or poor we each approximately benefit to the same degree as we contribute. If we all end up, roughly, where we start and social mobility is limited, the system is broken. Recent work with a social landlord revealed that the domestic finances of some tenants are such that in the event of any emergency (any non-routine expenditure), there is insufficient financial headroom for all debts to be paid when due. Something has to give, often the rent, and if not resolved very quickly, it establishes long-term indebtedness with insufficient financial resilience for the debtor to ever catch up. The ultimate consequence can be eviction and homelessness solving neither the problem of the debtor nor of the creditor.

Even for the relatively prosperous, there has been a substantial shift in recent years from ownership of things, which is enabled by and stimulates the accumulation of capital, to renting or hiring. There are a host of factors driving this shift, from lower security of employment to higher capital costs of assets, loss of tax breaks on some pension investments which disincentivise savings and easy availability of long-term credit at persistently low interest rates. In the UK these factors have been reflected in a shift in the balance of home-ownership versus renting down from around 71% in 2003 to 63% in 2018[7], from substantial acquisition of cars on hire-purchase agreements (a finite term contract at the end of which the purchaser normally owns the vehicle) to personal contract plans where the supplying manufacturer charges the customer for the proportion of value to be used up during their custodianship (in effect a rental agreement), with the customer either paying off the balance or returning the vehicle at the end of the agreement. Even mobile phones, increasingly powerful, increasingly expensive, are being sold on monthly terms. The effect of all of these changes on the individual is that they become increasingly reliant on regular income to keep servicing the debt while not accumulating any net value in the assets. They become trapped in a cycle of debt renewal and, unless fortunate or very well paid, are unable to accumulate any capital to escape the cycle. They become financially vulnerable to both maintained employment and the ability to service the debt. Learning about money, how to manage it and the consequences of financial decisions are critical as without financial resilience, all other aspects of life increase in fragility.

Networking for resilience

The final aspect of Lacy's model to consider is that of gaining strength and robustness from connections. Each individual is a node, not just in one but in many networks both horizontally through family, friends and peers and vertically through hierarchies of community or employment (Figure 3.2). These can give us strength or weakness, a sense of belonging or the feeling of being trapped. We are each the spider at the centre of our own particular web of relationships.

There is nothing in the structure of a network that determines it as being virtuous. Virtue (or not) is embedded in our behaviour and that of others. While for many the primary network is family, at least in childhood, this is far from universal and nor can family be necessarily claimed as a universal good if, as can be the case, it is not supportive. Our networks are commonly informal organisations, loosely structured not centrally directed, but nonetheless social hierarchy arises, leadership emerges and membership will have its costs and benefits. However, the networks may be comprised of family, neighbours, church or work and they should be enabling and encouraging. If they are, they will enhance personal resilience; if not

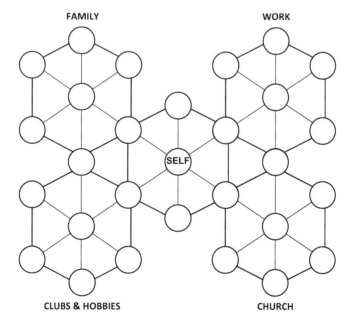

FIGURE 3.2   Peer network examples

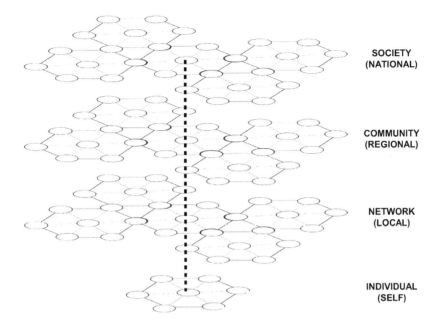

SOCIETY
(NATIONAL)

COMMUNITY
(REGIONAL)

NETWORK
(LOCAL)

INDIVIDUAL
(SELF)

FIGURE 3.3   Social hierarchy of networks

they may be damaging. Our immediate network is a nested system within other higher order networks (Figure 3.3), it will link to community (whether of race, religion, locality, common interest, ability or disability) and through that to wider society. The network is valuable not just for the support it provides but is the device through which each of us can establish a pathway to a different future. It is a mechanism that offers both the fundamental needs expressed in Maslow's hierarchy and a route through which we can self-actualise.

It seems that the foundations of resilience rest in the network infrastructure of supportive relationships and the meeting of our fundamental needs in terms of food, housing and finance. If those requirements are not met, it is unlikely there will be capacity for growth and aspiration in other aspects of life. It is difficult to address the question for individuals of how much resilience is enough, that will be a function of the set of nested relationships in which each of us is cradled and the extent to which we each draw from and contribute to those relationships. For each of us, there will be some trade-off, a cost-benefit balance achieved between the investment we choose to make in relationships and our level of resilience.

Resilient citizens and democracy

Resilient people will enable a properly functioning democracy, one in which each is free to make fully informed, autonomous, decisions constrained by belongingness, their membership of a wider society. Such people will engage in and adhere to a system of governance which has their informed consent and be fully engaged by and in the processes from which that governance arises. To ensure such engagement, a functioning democracy will require more than one layer of governance with a particular focus on localising decision-making, decentralising power. This gives operational meaning to the principle of subsidiarity, demanding that competence be developed at the level of the individual citizen. Decisions will need to be taken at different embedded levels (depending on the population affected and involved), some local, some regional and some national. This sort of distributed decision structure, differing in detail and execution, is common to most countries. What is also common and must be continuously resisted is the tendency of such systems to centralise driving the need to reassert and reinforce local control. This practical exercise in managing freedom is shown in Figure 3.4.

Resilient citizens, endowed with competence, will understand and be able to exercise their democratic obligations and privileges, comprehend their responsibilities to themselves and each other and accept the outcome of democratic processes. They will recognise that power is loaned by them to government and not devolved from it. The obligation on politicians (who are also citizens) is both to propose to the electorate policies and approaches that reflect the politician's views of the world and to listen to the wishes and desires of their electorate. An Intelligent Nation cannot emerge and be sustained if consent is withheld. Politicians are elected to carry out the processes of government on behalf of all citizens; they pitch for the

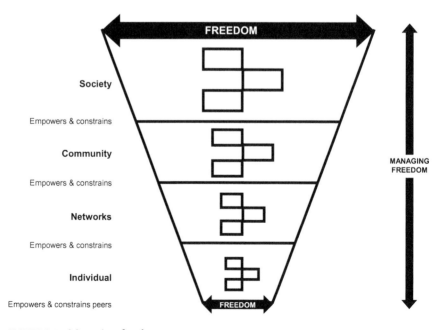

FIGURE 3.4 Managing freedom

job on the basis of a manifesto against which they must be held to account. Perhaps, if they cannot deliver on their manifesto, they should engage with the electorate on alternative choices. This is a deliberately naïve view, but it works when electors assert themselves.

Essential for an Intelligent Nation, what gives Government legitimacy is true democratic consent achieved through mass participation in electoral processes; every citizen with a vote must be able to use that vote. It requires both that there is authentic engagement and that citizens believe that their wishes, desires and hopes are being responded to. Given that the turnout for Presidential elections in the USA between 1908 and 2012 never exceeded 65.4%[8] with a 56.9%[9] turnout in 2016 and in the UK[10], a peak of 83.9% in 1950 and 67.3% in 2019, it seems a lot of people are not participating.

It is beyond the scope of this book to properly explore why this is the case but we should consider four possibilities. First is perhaps the lack of awareness, simple ignorance or fear of the process. Second is an active choice, a decision to abdicate from the responsibility of being a voter; 'If I don't vote what happens can't be my fault!' Third is disillusionment possibly reflecting the Irish saying that 'there is no point in voting, the government will get in anyway'. Fourth and most disturbing is that those in power, even in a democracy, become so divorced from the nation on whose behalf they govern, receive information so filtered and sanitised that it misleads, are so isolated by their advocates and disciples that they are unable to hear the protestations and objections of the citizens. Every capital has its political bubble; maybe the task of electors in a democracy is to burst it.

Ulrich (1983) proposes a methodology to address the misuse of power in decision-making and offers this as a step towards more transparent, engaged democracy. Beer (1994) and Checkland (1981) offer alternative approaches to encourage engagement rooted in relatively small or discrete groups. Recent dramatic changes in digital technology offer real opportunity for low cost, high impact, high speed engagement in decision-making. Employed primarily by online retailers and entertainment platforms, especially so-called 'reality TV', the response to the Coronavirus pandemic has seen a substantial growth in online communications. The same technology, subject to appropriate security and privacy for voters, offers a potential paradigm shift for public engagement in politics. Application of digital technologies to citizen engagement could support further devolution of certain powers, reinforcing local governance and enabling new alignments of service delivery such as the progressive integration of Health and Social Care in place-based services. This study starts to show what might be possible in adapting and redesigning service provision to meet local needs and re-engaging individuals and communities.

Adopting the ideas outlined by Murray demands an approach in which politicians create the conditions under which individuals make their own decisions, where services are integrated NOT for the purpose of reducing cost but to deliver greater benefit with less intrusion. The approach, based on exploitation of digital capability, must ensure that power rests in the hands of the individual citizen not exercised by an alternative, if local, set of politicians. These changes demand that

Why place-based policy is critical to the intelligent nation: Chris Murray

In a constantly changing world, one of the most challenging yet crucial questions for any modern state is how to remain relevant to their citizens at every spatial level from the global to the neighbourhood, thereby strengthening trust and maintaining a sense of social contract.

One response to this is a gradual shift toward decentralisation, from Japan to Chile, France to Finland. Some systems – Germany is perhaps most often cited – are historically decentralised and have been looked to for inspiration, particularly by the UK, one of the most centralised states in the developed world. It is ironic then that the post-war German state was broken up and federalised at the insistence of the British, whose experience of Empire dictated that centralised equalled strong, federal weak; a model that has been flipped upside down by modern economic forces, with which we are now playing catch-up.

Yet even the most decentralised systems are struggling to deal with some highly complex 21st Century challenges, for example, climate change, increasing wealth gaps or social cohesion; all issues that national programmes have largely failed to resolve.

What is place-based policy?

Building on localism and a series of 'devolution deals' in the UK, a different policy response is emerging, described as 'place-based'. This approach takes a defined geography for a specific set of issues, then assesses the totality of national and local resources, services, programmes and agencies who work directly upon or influence that issue. It then asks: if we were going to design this system from scratch, what would it look like? How could we best deploy the combined sum of our resource to have greatest impact?

In reality, this thinking has been around for a while. The Total Place and then Whole Area programmes among others made assessments of the total public spend in a locality and how that might be used to achieve better outcomes, for example, for health, inequality and employment.

But if we are honest, very little progress was ever made on implementation, and only now are we seeing relatively modest steps forward.

One thing we can be certain of is that place – in the sense of where and how we live – really matters and impacts on us economically, physically and emotionally, for better or worse. Understanding its importance is therefore critical to the evolution of the Intelligent Nation.

Why place is important

A meaningful geography – e.g. a travel to work or functioning economic area around a city region – offers a coherent spatial level at which to organise specific sets of services: transport; skills and employment; health and social care; housing; economic development.

Delivering services at this level can allow for a detailed and nuanced understanding of distinctive local needs. For example, the differences in life expectancy of 10 or more years between neighbourhoods within several UK cities is a clear indicator that instead of avoiding a post-code lottery, nationally delivered place-blind approaches actually create one.

Places are global hubs. Nation states set the parameters – e.g. trade deals and tariffs – but flows of labour, goods and commerce are in reality between places, mainly cities. The American urbanist Bruce Katz goes further, stating that there is really no such thing as a national economy any more, and instead flows between big cities define fluid and porous international economic boundaries.

A focus on place can support positive community identity. For example, cities seem to have an ability to give coherence to multiple and complex sets of identities that nations often fail to do. Providing places, or rather the people that live in them, with increased autonomy can also enhance local pride and confidence, getting solutions closer to problems at the same time.

Not only has a centralised and siloed system no realistic chance of aligning services in a locally relevant manner to capitalise on the nature and strengths of place, but different parts of such a system will unwittingly undermine each other.

The point is more fundamental than whether any one policy will work or not, it is that all policies will struggle to deliver results because they are unable, as the system stands, to view or address issues in the round. We can see this in several UK policy areas, with the Health and Social Care systems of England offering a clear example (these being integrated within Scotland).

Health and social care integration: Place-based policy in action

Reductions in local authority funding overall have impacted significantly on Adult Social Care services. Preventative services, particularly for the elderly, that kept people in their homes and out of hospital are now at a bare minimum. This means more people are admitted to hospital, placing an increased burden on the NHS. The systemic response from NHS is to overspend to meet the immediate need and call on government to fill the gap, which over time could amount to much more funding than was originally removed from local authorities, robbing Peter to pay Paul.

Providing care for people in their own home costs an average of around £300 per week, £650 in a care home, but £2,800 to keep someone in a hospital bed when this care fails, and the longer an elderly person is in hospital, the harder it is for them to return to their home and previous routine.

This is a market failure of significant proportions and a place-based approach is required to address it. If these services were locally integrated funds could be diverted to prevention, saving the NHS and the public purse overall across the long term. If those services could then be locally tailored to focus on the specific kinds of prevention needed across each place, then even better results and even less spending would result.

This theory is now being tested in the Greater Manchester Health Social Care Partnership, with the devolution of £6billion into local hands, agreed in 2015, with implementation from 2016. All NHS trusts, local authorities and other care providers are obliged to co-commission into a legally binding local framework, based on local knowledge and evidence, and led by a local partnership board.

Taking into account set up time, four years is insufficient to truly assess the results of such an ambitious and complex programme, but evidence is emerging with more expected in the coming year. This suggests the programme is working, with significant results on prevention and stopping people falling into dependence on services, less so on changing the results of treatments once people are in that position, but that alone feels like a big success.

Other smaller integration programmes are taking place across England through the Better Care Fund. The roll-out of the BCF was criticised by the National Audit Office for being over-optimistic in its stated aims, relatively small scale compared to the size of the problem and particularly for not reducing 'bed blocking' – getting people out of hospital quickly once they are admitted.

An 'emotionally' Intelligent Nation? Sharing power, building trust

Building on these pilots, the UK could completely revolutionise its public services through a place-based approach. Austerity has impacted on Whitehall as well as City Hall and it seems nonsensical to still try and run large swathes of local services from the national level. Elements of transport, health, housing, skills, employment, climate change, air quality and many other policy areas could be operated in a place-based manner. The fact they are not means we probably have the question the wrong way around. Instead of asking, why should this service or fund be decentralised, perhaps we should ask, why is it not decentralised? Issues of accountability, capacity and other barriers all have pragmatic solutions.

And if a State really wanted to empower people and gain their trust, they might even consider allowing them to retain some of the taxes they pay at the local level, spending them on what they think is right for their place. That however is currently a rather distant dream in the UK, with around only 9% of all taxes raised locally retained locally, compared to 35% in Germany, 50% in the US and a whopping 80% in Tokyo (although the size of a middling country).

> Yet at least one survey has focused on another fundamental issue that must be addressed in health social care – or any other public service – integration. Not one of structures, funding or even objectives, but one of trust between the key players.
>
> This is highly relevant to the question set out at the start of this case study, and the answer is perhaps that we also need an 'emotionally' Intelligent Nation. One that understands that, in the same way it has to broker and share power internationally to gain relevance and win trust, it must do the same back home, through an appreciation of place. That: a sharing of power below the national level is a strengthening, not a weakening of the State; its apparatus can become more efficient and effective; and it can gain relevance to the daily lives of its citizens by doing so.

new models of democratic engagement emerge and inform policy at local, regional and national levels and rely on completion of deployment of high-speed internet connectivity and digital devices. Enhancing democratic participation may offer the strongest moral case for the practical challenge of eliminating digital poverty and exclusion. There are of course ethical, legal and practical considerations to be explored and resolved in this regard but it would seem at best careless not to address the opportunity. It might offer means of enhancing trust in government and the state while promoting privacy, freedom and shared values.

What is the purpose of government?

Why does a nation of intelligent resilient citizens need a government? If the rhetoric of self-organisation and distributed power is to be relied upon then maybe government is redundant? However, the capacity for self-regulating which emerges in a natural system needs to be created in an artificial one, so what do we want government to do for us?

The traditional answer has been 'Defence of the Realm' and, in the UK, the Defence of the Realm Act (1914) was passed for that purpose. It gave the government the powers and responsibilities it thought necessary to deal with the challenges of the day. While the contemporary world and international relationships are very different to those of 1914, the perceived threats from the 2020 Coronavirus Covid-19 pandemic, and some governmental responses to it internationally, suggest that some similarly draconian, population-controlling measures have been put in place. Dentchev et al. (2015) regard the question as 'under-explored' while Heywood (2004) asserts that 'most people accept without question that government is necessary, assuming that without it orderly and civilised existence would be impossible' Citing Hobbes 'Leviathan', Heywood avers that without government 'Society would descend into a civil war of 'every man against every man', while in considering liberty Hayek (2006) suggests that 'Coercion, however, cannot be altogether avoided, because the only way to prevent it is by the threat of coercion'. He suggests that free society has countered this by 'conferring the monopoly of coercion on the state' thereafter limiting the power of the state to preventing coercion by individuals.

Perhaps the role of government is to inhibit interference in the affairs of any one citizen by any other, to create conditions that enable safe interactions of all types and arrange the provision of social and fundamental infrastructures, regulating (including sound money) and preventing potentially coercive or inequitable commercial and other engagements. Importantly, it can represent its citizens in relationships with the governments of other countries. The government exists by the consent of the citizen to preserve the freedom of the citizen including the power to change the government. This provides organisational closure and affirms the role of the democratic process.

Freedom to change the government requires a democratic system, and Bakunin (2008) warns of the tendency of government to self-preserve, to become pathologically autopoietic, suggesting that even 'a scientific body to which had been confided the government of society would soon end by no longer occupying itself with science at all, but with quite another business; and that business, the business of all established powers, would be to perpetuate itself by rendering the society confided to its care ever more stupid and consequently more in need of its government and direction'. It is essential therefore that there is an effective stewardship of the rules of governance, a means by which the demos can assert their right to elect and remove governments. One way in which this might be assisted would be to restrict funding of political parties to fees paid by individual members so that no individual or organisation could acquire influence through financial means. With every individual having one vote in elections, it seems equitable that every individual should have the influence of one vote on the policies of a political party along with the absolute right to support none of them, financially or otherwise. Party survival would then depend upon their ability to attract members to contribute to their cause, generating a more constructive and consultative relationship between citizens and citizen-politicians.

The period since 1914 has seen the emergence and dissolution of the Union of Soviet Socialist Republics (USSR), the emergence of the European Union (EU) and other inter-country co-operation blocs, the World Bank, the United Nations (UN) and the defence led North Atlantic Treaty Organisation (NATO). A shift to global markets and trade with global supply chains has been signalled through, among others, the North American Free Trade Agreement (NAFTA), the Trans-Pacific Partnership, the European Free Trade Association, the World Trade Organisation and the General Agreement on Tariffs and Trade (GATT). There is an Intergovernmental Panel on Climate Change (IPCC) seeking to assess the science on climate change and advise governments accordingly on policies and actions. The fragility and tenuous nature of some of those arrangements is always under scrutiny and they have all been tested. Flights and trade were disrupted by climate-related events such as the eruption in 2010 of Eyjafjallajökull in Iceland and floods in Thailand, while the 2011 nuclear plant failure at Fukushima, Japan, following a tsunami disrupted energy supply affecting production and exports. There have been political changes such as the 2016 decision by the people of the UK, finally implemented in 2020, that the country should leave the European Union with all that entails. The Coronavirus Covid-19 has not only led to the so called lockdown of significant populations (many millions across Europe) but has affected global trade, business volumes and value, with entertainment, sporting and religious events cancelled and an inevitable global recession. In addressing this challenge, international arrangements come under pressure. Kern[11] notes that the European Union through the European Central Bank purchased government debt relating to other European Union member countries only to be challenged by the German Constitutional Court in which Judge Peter Michael Huber asserted: 'As long as we don't live in a European super-state, a country's membership is governed by its constitutional law' with German Parliament member Klaus-Peter Willsch saying 'One thing should never be forgotten: Europe is not a federal state, but a legal community developed from the founding core of an economic community in clearly limited areas of national sovereignty. Any sovereignty of the European Union is only derived from the sovereignty of the constituent member states'. Clearly, there is a need to sustain the rights of citizens for self-governance, to limit the tendency of bureaucracies to over-reach their powers and to preserve international cooperation. Meanwhile highly efficient global supply chains struggle because they are low in resilience with narrow sources of supply, limited in-process stock and lack flexibility to cope with rapid and substantial demand shifts; that is not how they were conceived to work. This emphasises the need for an Intelligent Nation to comprehend its interdependency with others and for its government to ensure, as a minimum, that the critical needs of its population can be met from within its own civil rather than military sovereign capability or a secure supply chain.

The complexity, rate of change and scale of challenge suggests it is time to reconsider the role and organisation of government. The functional, bureaucratic, input-oriented and non-adaptive mechanisms of the past seem unsuited to the future we are creating. In an Intelligent Nation defence of the realm moves beyond the important but narrow concern of the military sphere to embrace all those characteristics of the nation and the state which will render it capable of continued independent existence. Independent is perhaps not right, as every nation exists in a state of cooperation and co-dependence with other nations and is nested in a natural, commercial and political environment, self-determining is more apt. As the German example just cited suggests, any country must be free to make its own decisions, to make its own choices but must do so with awareness of the consequences for its relationships with others and it must do so in a way which supports its viability. Such self-determination requires resilience, the capability to absorb shocks, perturbations and disruptions and to rapidly recover from them. Resilience needs to be sustained (and sustainable) across both social and fundamental infrastructure embracing all activities and supporting the resilience of each individual citizen.

Model for an Intelligent Nation

When all of the argument of the current chapter is brought together, it provides a model for an Intelligent Nation, one in which power is always located at the right level, which is decentralised as much as possible and centralised as much as necessary. It recognises the right of the citizens to choose how they are governed while the citizens accept the legitimacy of that governance as granted by themselves.

The key demand by resilient citizens is to be supported and enabled by government and the social and fundamental infrastructure services it provides, either directly or through funding of third-party operators. This in turn enables the resilience of each citizen, family, network, community from which can emerge an Intelligent Nation. The desired outcome of the government activity should be to support the optimal independence of each citizen. Citizens who are educated, healthy, skilled, fed, housed can be responsible for themselves, for obeying the law (that they will have created), for exercising their democratic rights and responsibilities and will recognise the obligation to do so. They will create, sometimes with support, homes, networks and communities. How should we design social infrastructure, in large part our public services, to support and enable this?

Figure 3.5 brings all of the elements together in a single representation showing how the network levels identified in Figure 3.3 map to four different levels of government, from the self, through local and regional to national. The Intelligent Nation has the individual citizen at its root and interactions by individuals generate the hierarchy of networks communities and society, each requiring different levels of governance. Each level of governance, from self-management through to national government, is constrained by the level of governance in which it is embedded, each evaluating its position, interpreting it and exercising authority over its contained levels. While the placing of the boundaries between these levels will be explored in subsequent chapters, they must respect issues of location and belongingness, and both economic and social cohesion.

Ultimate power is retained by the individual citizen because, through the electoral process, they create democratic closure, electing and deposing levels of government as they see fit through the electoral processes. All of this is embedded in two overlapping and interdependent infrastructural systems. The first, social infrastructure is the system of commerce, education, healthcare, civil administration and defence; these are the mechanisms of value generation at the level of the nation. The second is the underpinning fundamental infrastructure of energy, waste, water, transport and information and communications technology, the value-enabling services and artefacts without which the system cannot function efficiently or effectively to support the population. There are interdependencies both between the elements at each level and between the social and fundamental levels. These must be recognised and their interfaces managed.

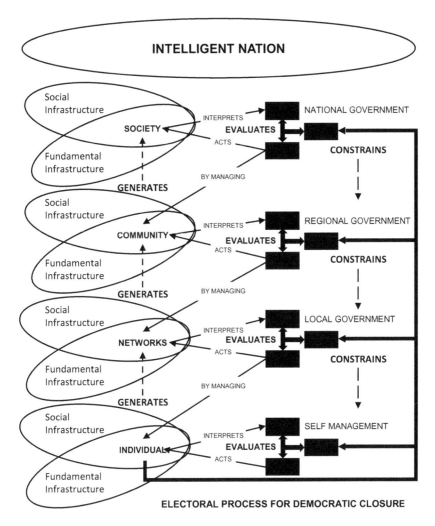

FIGURE 3.5 Model for an Intelligent Nation

Summary

Resilient citizens, aggregating to comprise an Intelligent Nation, will need an intelligent state to support and enable them. Enhancing democracy by investing in and developing the capability of each citizen to participate and contribute will require new ways of arranging services provided by or through the State; the established bureaucratic, functional organisations will not suffice. It will be essential to reorient to new models of delivery based on exploitation of digital capability and understanding of the outcomes required by and for the citizens. Social Infrastructure will need to be distributed, led by policies which are both central and local, allowing autonomous local action while maintaining the coherence of a whole nation policy where appropriate, always generating tensions which will need to be managed. As an Intelligent Organisation, the state will need to recognise that its primary role is to enable value for people and organisations, to create the circumstances under which they can generate value for themselves. The citizen will be at the centre of the thinking; services will be designed to maximise the value added to them and minimise the demand of the state upon them whether through time, taxation or other restriction. As far as possible, the state must aim for a single point of contact with each citizen and that single point of contact acting as an interface to services designed around their needs. Services and state provision will need to be designed to reduce dependency and their success measured not simply by budgetary compliance but primarily by achievement of the desired outcomes, the most critical of which is perhaps the reduction in the need for state provision. The ultimate performance measure of the state should perhaps be the extent to which by enabling citizens and supporting their capability it makes itself redundant.

The emergent property of the system comprised of intelligent citizens is society or, as I have called it earlier, the Intelligent Nation. In the next chapter, we will explore how an Intelligent Nation creates the shape of an intelligent state.

Key points

- Intelligent Nation needs intelligent citizens;
- Citizens create the culture, values and beliefs that underpin the state;
- Individual is the heart of a nation, its source of current and future value;
- Every individual is of equal potential and must receive equal opportunity;
- Support must be available to all and it is the responsibility of the powerful, influential and privileged to create opportunities for others;
- Power is historically grossly disbalanced between the individual and the state;
- In an Intelligent Nation, the primacy of the individual not the state as the generator of power and wealth must be asserted;
- Politicians are invited to exercise power on behalf of the citizens at whose behest they continue in office;
- Each citizen must conceive of themselves as an Intelligent Organisation, able to generate and enable value, to nurture their identity and use information to be their best self, learning and adapting in the light of new information;
- Each citizen exhibits five characteristics of personal resilience: Perspective, Emotional Intelligence, Purpose and Values, Connections and Physical Energy;
- Each citizen exists in multiple layered networks, contributing to and benefitting from them at personal (family, work, clubs) and local, regional and national levels;
- Resilient people enable a properly functioning democracy in which they loan their power to government (at all levels) to exercise on their behalf.

- The purpose of government is to sustain the viability of the country in concert with the people;
- Ultimately, power belongs to the individual citizens who collectively create government through engagement in the democratic process.

References

Ackoff, R.L., (1981) *Creating the Corporate Future*, Wiley, New York

Bakunin, M., (2008) *Dieu et l'État*, L'Altiplano, France

Beckford, J., (1994) *Entropy and Entrepreneurship: The Centralisation of Capital as a Barrier to Innovatory Behaviour*, Entrepreneurship, Innovation and Change, Vol. 3 No. 1, Plenum, New York

Beckford, J., (2020) *The Intelligent Organisation: Driving Systemic Change with Information*, 2nd edition, Routledge, London

Beer, S., (1994) *Beyond Dispute, The Invention of Team Syntegrity*, Wiley, Chichester, UK

Checkland, P.B., (1981) *Systems Thinking, Systems Practice*, Wiley, Chichester, UK

Dentchev, N., Haezendonck, E. & van Balen, M. (2015) The role of governments in the business and society debate, *Business & Society*, Vol. 56. doi:10.1177/0007650315586179

Hammer, M. & Champy, J., (1993) *Reengineering the Corporation*, Nicholas Brealey, London

Handy, C., (1990) *The Age of Unreason*, Arrow, London

Hayek, F.A., (2006) *The Constitution of Liberty*, Routledge Classics, London

Herzberg, F. Mauser, B. & Synderman, B.B., (1959) *The Motivation to Work*, 2nd edition, Wiley, New York

Heywood, A., (2004) *Political Theory, An Introduction*, Palgrave MacMillan, Basingstoke, UK

Hills, J., (2015) *Good Times, Bad Times*, Policy Press, UK

Hills, R., (2016) *Emotional Resilience in Business*, Authority Guide, UK

Kahnemann, D., (2011) *Thinking, Fast and Slow*, Penguin, UK

Lewin, K., (1947) Frontiers in group dynamics: Concept, method and reality in social science; equilibrium and social change, *Human Relations*, Vol. 1, No 1, pp. 5–41.

Maddocks, J., (2014) *Emotional Intelligence @Work*, Spa, Gloucestershire, UK

Mandela, N., (1995) *The Long Walk to Freedom'*, Little Brown & Co., New York

Maslow, A., (1970) *Motivation and Personality*, 2nd edition, Harper and Row, New York

Mischel, W., (2014) *The Marshmallow Test*, Bantam Press, Random House, London

Murray, C., (2019) States of mind, *RSA Journal*, Vol. 2, pp. 10–15, Royal Society for the Arts, London

Nobbs, D., (2009) *The Reginald Perrin Omnibus*, Arrow, London

Peters, S., (2012) *The Chimp Paradox*, Vermilion, Random House, London

Seddon, J., (2008) *Systems Thinking in the Public Sector*, Triarchy Press, Axminster, UK

Startz, D., (2010) *Profit of Education*, Praeger, ABC-CLIO, California

Taleb, N., (2010) *The Black Swan*, Penguin, London

Ulrich, W., (1983) *Critical Heuristics of Social Planning*, Haupt Verlag, Berne

Notes

1. https://www.mckinsey.com/business-functions/organization/our-insights/motivating-people-getting-beyond-money 17/02/2020
2. https://www.hrmagazine.co.uk/article-details/five-steps-to-personal-resilience 19/02/2020

3. https://blog.lboro.ac.uk/sbe/2016/03/02/another-fine-mess/ 18/02/2020
4. http://intelligentorganisation.com/uncategorised/university-challenged/ 19/02/2020
5. www.newsroom.co.nz/2020/02/13/1032108/housing-policy 20/02/2020
6. https://www.bbc.co.uk/news/health-40927705 20/02/2020
7. https://www.bbc.co.uk/news/business-47070020 16/06/2020
8. https://www.statista.com/statistics/262915/voter-turnout-in-the-us-presidential-elections/ 22/02/2020
9. https://www.vox.com/policy-and-politics/2016/11/10/13587462/trump-election-2016-voter-turnout 22/02/2020
10. http://www.ukpolitical.info/Turnout45.htm 22/02/2020
11. https://www.gatestoneinstitute.org/16031/germany-sovereignty-eu 20/05/2020

4

SOCIAL INFRASTRUCTURE AND SERVICES TO THE PUBLIC

Introduction

'Society' is an emergent product of the interactions of the citizens of an Intelligent Nation with each other and with the vertically and horizontally distributed social and fundamental infrastructures. Consistent with the idea of management being embedded in the process structures of an organisation, the synthesis of nation and infrastructure systems requires an intermediary unifying and organising mechanism. On the individual level, that device emerges informally through relationships, families, streets and tribes; for communities, regions and a whole country, it requires greater formality. The arbitrating body needs to be legitimate in the eyes of the population; its administrative activity must be objective, free of bias and individual conflicts of interest. We call the legitimate body government (at different levels) and the administrative activity (in all its dimensions), governance. Government and governance of an Intelligent Nation require a purposeful and resilient infrastructure eco-system and a systemic approach to efficiency and effectiveness in order to formulate appropriate structural arrangements for delivery of public services.

Design for a resilient infrastructure ecosystem

Our networks of relationships are embedded in two interdependent, interacting infrastructure sub-systems: the fundamental and the social. This chapter will set the context through a model of both before focusing on social infrastructure. Figure 4.1 was developed in 2009 for UK Government research into infrastructure interdependency[1]. There are a variety of approaches to choosing the sectors, none definitive. The UK Centre for the Protection of National Infrastructure[2] names 13 national infrastructure sectors: Chemicals, Civil Nuclear, Communications, Defence, Emergency Services, Energy, Finance, Food, Government, Health, Space, Transport and Water with some having 'sub-sectors'.

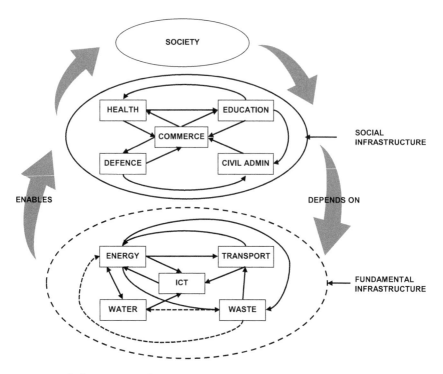

FIGURE 4.1 Infrastructure sub-systems

While Rinaldi et al. (2001) list eight: Telecommunications, Electric, Gas and Oil, Banking and Finance, Transportation, Water, Government Services and Emergency Services; the USA[3] identifies sixteen, including Chemical, Commercial Facilities, Communications, Critical Manufacturing, Dams, Defence, Emergency Services, Energy, Finance, Food and Agriculture, Government Facilities, Healthcare and Public Health, Information Technology, Nuclear, Transportation and Water along with a number of sector-specific agencies. The European Union Directive 2008/114/EC (2008) on critical infrastructure protection concerns itself only with energy (Electricity, Gas, Oil) and Transport (Road, Rail, Air and Water), whereas France[4] takes an interesting approach, clustering its multiple sectors around four key areas of responsibility rather than functions. These areas are basic human needs of food, water management and health; sovereign needs of civilian, legal and military activities; economic needs for energy, finance and transport; and a technological area dealing with communication, technologies broadcasting, industry, space and research.

It is the interdependence and interactions of the sub-systems that is of most interest; teased apart for the purposes of illustration our lived experience of them is that they are inextricably intertwined. The Intelligent Nation is enabled by effective governance of a complex nest of persistent and non-linear information loops through which fundamental infrastructure enables social infrastructure, from which emerges society which then depends on the social infrastructure which depends on the fundamental. Operationally, the individual elements are so closely interdependent that for many purposes they might be regarded as a single system. However, while we must recognise the fundamental and social infrastructure as a whole system, there is a distinction between their purposes that allows us to imagine a porous boundary around the fundamental infrastructure and separate it out for now. It is the social infrastructure that provides services directly addressing personal needs.

Social infrastructure

Considered from the perspective of the Intelligent Nation, the social infrastructure is both value enabling and venue generating, the distinction resting on the particular purpose being served. Education, for example, might be primarily considered as value enabling, it helps to create the future for citizens, while the emergency department of a hospital is value generating, managing the present. Within each and every element of the social infrastructure, there is a need to comprehend the contribution the particular service element makes and design it accordingly.

Social infrastructure services are predominantly provided to individuals through government or government-appointed providers addressing education, health and social care, civil administration (including policing and criminal justice), housing, defence, taxation (national and local revenues) and benefits (financial support). Commercial enterprises, conventionally value generating, are largely owned independently of government in many countries but are tightly tied into government policy through taxation, regulation, incentives, grants and investment arrangements reflecting Braithwaite's (2008) regulated capitalism. In some countries, governments at all levels hold strategic commercial, value-generating investments in selected industries and while the Intelligent Nation neither necessitates nor precludes private, public, community or state-based commercial ownership models, it does recognise that the State must provide some regulation of commercial activity for the defence of itself and protection of its citizens.

Social infrastructure services must provide appropriate support throughout life and enable individual resilience, maximising the value enabled, minimising disruption to the citizen. Appropriately supportive interventions means liberation from dependency on the State and altered life trajectories, and the 'return' to society from such intervention is measured through more extensive education, improved health, sustained employment and greater life expectancy with a good outcome so that a net recipient of support can become a net contributor to society. To achieve this, the State must offer services designed to meet the outcomes required by each citizen equally, regardless of age, gender, sexuality, religion, economic or other differences or circumstances. Understanding value must take account of the long-term systemic value of provision and we must include in any evaluation those costs imparted to the environment and to the citizen as service user. Each different location will need services modified to reflect the highly distributed model of Intelligent Nation. The circumstances of a citizen in any given location are unique to them and equity in service should be about providing the support required to achieve the desired outcome, not equality of inputs. One size only ever fits all badly, one size will always be systemically inefficient, inequitable and ineffective.

The Intelligent Nation question to be asked is not 'what can we devolve from the centre' but rather 'what cannot be delivered locally'? The presumption should be in favour of local, even ultra-local provision and as far as possible invert the debate around localisation. An Intelligent Nation reasserts the idea of subsidiarity, that is, each decision should be taken at the lowest organisational level that the competence exists. After many years of a centralising and functionalist approach, achievement of a radical decentralising approach will require substantial realignment of decision powers and authorities (the legal competences) accompanied by a distribution of resources and a massive cultural and behavioural shift.

A substantial and complex problem that exemplifies the challenge in the UK is to structure and organise policing within Peelian principles while meeting the demands of local versus regional and national policing. The political context is that Police and Crime Commissioners have the power to establish local policy and allocate resources to activities across defined geographical areas while the Home Office, with national responsibility, cannot 'mandate' particular approaches or technologies; the tensions between the two hampering interoperability and information exchange.

Scale and change: Mr. Chris Singer (NPCC, Rtd)

The first duty of government is to keep its citizens safe and the country secure. That duty is discharged externally by the deployment of armed forces and internally, through the security apparatus of policing, secret intelligence services and latterly the National Crime Agency, an organisation that attempts to bridge national and local capability.

Since 1285 what is now the UK has delivered policing in one form or another, replacing old systems with new as society and threat has changed and with it the need for different forms of control. Sir Robert Peel in 1828, concerned at increasing crime and believing that 'security for property, and even for person – but particularly the security for property, is not what it ought to be in every well-regulated society'[5] sought leave for a Parliamentary Committee to be formed to examine the issue which found that established systems of night watches and volunteer constables were ineffective. A year later Peel's Metropolitan Police Bill received assent establishing a full time professional and centrally organised Police Force of uniformed constables.

By 1851 around 13,000 Constables across England and Wales operated in towns and rural areas and in 1856 the establishment of rural forces became mandatory. Where counties or boroughs had already established a force or established a new and efficient force, then one quarter of the costs of pay and clothing for constables were met by the Treasury. However, if a borough with a population of less than 5,000 maintained a separate police force then they received no financial support, encouraging smaller forces to consolidate with the county police.

This development of policing centralising and adapting to new populations and patterns of crime has continued. The Police Act of 1964 allowed the amalgamation of forces into more efficient units and over the subsequent decade 117 forces reduced to 49. Latterly alliances have been formed between forces and the National Crime Agency (NCA) with its supporting network of Regional Organised Crime Units (ROCU) was introduced in 2013. Introducing the agency, Theresa May said it was being introduced, along with other measures, to remove a 'tendency to operate in silos' and provide national mechanisms to allocate officers and other police resources along with coordinated border policing to fight the most serious policeable threats facing the country.

The entrenched tendency to operate in silos in relation to serious organised crime has been addressed at least in part through the creation and use of the Strategic Policing Requirement (SPR), with power given to the Director General of the NCA, responsible for reducing serious and organised crime, to direct Chief Constables and the role played by ROCUs. The SPR sets out the national threats that the police must prepare for and the appropriate national policing capabilities that are required to counter them. Serious and Organised Crime is one such threat. As a result, each force must commit resources to addressing it with the Director General of the NCA holding binding powers to direct local forces to take action. ROCUs provide a means of prioritising co-ordinated action between local forces and the NCA ensuring that they act collectively to counter threats and coordinating nationally to prevent 'blue-on-blue' events when, working in isolation, they compromise each other.

Threats do not stand still, they evolve. Police officers know that there are more organised crime groups operating in the UK than ever before, those groups have changed and become networks rather than groups headed by a 'crime boss'. Internet enabled crime has allowed domestic and international criminals to exploit opportunity, enabling the exploitation of vulnerable individuals including children and greatly increasing the cost of crime to the UK economy. This includes the creation of and access to images showing abuse and even the 'live abuse' of children and other vulnerable people streamed to audiences online.

The March 2018 National Security Capability Review[6] states

> Serious and organised crime presents an increased and sustained threat to our security and prosperity.
>
> (Cabinet Office, 2018)

It identifies that organised crime impacts on public services, infrastructure and reputation through such things as ransomware, denial of service attacks, hacking and fraud. Where globalisation and technological change has benefitted business by opening up markets, making procurement simple and placing customers in reach of every supplier, those same changes have enabled criminal networks to grow and become more resilient simply as a result of their ability to operate in loose knit forms, where the loss of one member is unlikely to compromise the entire network. Their financial gains are so substantial that they are able to procure technology to assist and hide their activities, their scale equivalent to many legitimate small businesses. This picture is no different for the UK than it is for any other country where internet access is widespread, readily available and operating with little state regulation.

While these changes have taken place, individual police forces have struggled to cope with the twin impacts of austerity and rising demand. Austerity has stripped away not only police resource but also capacity in supporting agencies such as social care and housing. Rising demand comes from increased levels of crime, the need to safeguard the most vulnerable and investigations where policing persists in 'using 20th-century methods to try to cope with 21st-century technology'.[7]

Endless debate about structure, the effort and resource expended in pursuing one set of arrangements to only then abandon those arrangements and pursue a different structure is not serving the public, and allows criminals, who operate without bureaucratic organisational or national borders, to exploit the hiatus and flourish.

It is against this backdrop that policing must look to the future, innovate and adapt. The National Police Chiefs Council Vision 2025[8] calls for a more sophisticated response from a service that must adapt to the modern policing environment to meet community's needs. That sophisticated response needs to go far wider than debate about structure. An evolving criminal threat is not constrained by debate about command and control but is free roving and capable of mutating, adapting to exploit new opportunities and unconstrained by convention and tradition. To fight against that type of threat, policing needs to move away from an operating model that constrains to one that enables a more effective response. It must develop new effective means of countering threat and develop ways to make that efficient. It will need to be looking outward not inward, keeping the mission, fulfilment of purpose in sight at all times. That purpose continues to be making communities safer by upholding the law fairly and firmly; preventing crime and antisocial behaviour; keeping the peace; protecting and reassuring communities; investigating crime and bringing offenders to justice. Innovating to adopt new technology and lessen transactional processes, truly reducing the administrative burden to free resource for purposeful uses, embracing commissioning as a means of accessing capacity and capability without owning it, all offer opportunity to maximise effect and benefit from economies of scale.

In a report reviewing the difference a re-investment in policing numbers could make, Deloitte states 'The challenge is that while there is strong consensus that the current systems of national decision-making and delivery are failing in many areas, there is little consensus on alternative governance and structural solution'[9]. That consensus must be found and may rest in 'the outcome for the customer' (Beckford, 2017) which, for policing, must be the delivery of a service that achieves the mission it has set for itself. Policing must seek to build resilience, decrease threat and exploit opportunity, giving regard to the fact that the threats faced do not respect the boundaries of our communities.

This study demonstrates the challenge faced in designing services to be simultaneously local, regional, national, consistent and personalised and highlights the work to be undertaken to create a shared future. The bureaucratic nature of public services is also exposed here, the challenge of embedding adaptation in an organisation which depends on hierarchy for its functioning is made plain. This is not unique to policing.

A helpful analogy for challenges of this complexity may be natural eco-systems which when diverse and adaptive are resilient, having capacity to sustain themselves and recover from adversity; they are effective in securing their own survival. Discussing such systems Lomborg (2004) citing Ehrenfeld says 'if our ancestors had left us the ecological devastation we are leaving our descendants, our options for enjoyment, perhaps even for survival, today would be quite limited'. Barrow (2006) describes ecosystems management as adhering to a holistic view, critical to informing the management of complex societies and economies. Understanding how natural complex systems sustain themselves offers insights to how we might manage man-made systems. Lovelock (2019) building on his previous work (1995) points out the threat from failure, describing The Great Dying, '90 percent of marine species and 70 percent of land organisms were extinguished. Ecosystems did not recover for 30 million years'. Nature and natural systems and organisms, distributed, diverse, random, effective in pursuit of survival perhaps more than they are efficient, are resilient even if recovery is prolonged and individual species are extinct. Nature takes time but, as long as an entity is adapting with the changing environment, it can recover however much it is perturbed. In thinking about the design of an Intelligent Nation, we need to embrace the natural approaches of distributed decision-making, diversity, randomness and inefficiency in order to achieve the higher order goal of survival. We need to recognise that any artificial system needs to be designed to learn and adapt, to co-evolve with its environment, that any system which defines itself as 'knowing the answer' can only ever be wrong.

Systemic efficiency

Now that we have an understanding of the total eco-system of the Intelligent Nation, we need to think about its systemic effectiveness and efficiency.

Efficiency is conventionally defined as the measure of useful work done as a proportion of the resources employed, that is, for every set of inputs, there are two outputs, work and waste. Efficiency is the (energy) resource output, divided by the (energy) resource input expressed as a percentage. Ohno (1988), discussing the Toyota Production System, suggests that 'we use the word "efficiency" when talking about production, management and business. "Efficiency" … means cost reduction'. He goes on to suggest that 'improving efficiency only makes sense when tied to cost reduction' and that 'we have to start producing things using minimum manpower'. The design of a complete system of work and all the resources employed, including labour, required for its delivery, is a key determinant of the amount of useful work done. Anything not used productively is by Ohno's measure 'waste' and he sees this in overproduction, waiting time, transportation, processing activity, stock, movement and defective products or errors. However, when a narrow view of a process is taken, the local efficiency improvement can be deceptive. Limits to thinking inherently limit performance as the following case shows.

Hidden waste: Dr. John Beckford

A short(ish) blog this week –and, for reasons that will become clear, please don't print it!

I was invited by a University Professor (UP) to give a talk to Masters Students on the subject of Intelligent Organisation. Travelling by car I asked that a parking space be held for me – parking being notoriously difficult in and around Universities.

A process, roughly as follows, ensues:

Email from JB to UP: Could you book me a parking space please?

Email from UP to Reception: Please book a Parking Space for JB on <Date, Time>

Email from Reception to UP: Place X has been reserved for JB, please send these instructions

Email from UP to JB: Place X has been reserved for you, please follow these instructions

Email from JB to UP: Thank you

On arrival at the Car Park, Place X is occupied by a builder's van, so I park my car in Place Y

Following the received instructions, I enter the rear of the building, walk through the building to the reception desk.

JB 'Hello, I am JB, Parking place X was reserved for me but was occupied so I have parked in Parking place Y'

Receptionist 'Hello, thank you, I had better amend the paperwork or the parking attendant may ticket you'

Receptionist proceeds to amend a PAPER record and issues JB with a Plasticised Paper Hangar to place in the car showing amended Parking Place number, date and duration of stay. Assumption that the paper record is, somehow, shared with the parking attendant so that it can be checked.

JB 'Thank You' and walk back through the building to place the hangar in the front of the car.

JB Re-enters building and sets off to find host.

So far, 5 emails, two long walks (and yes, I know exercise is good for me) and two pieces of paper (assuming none of the emails were printed), one of which is plasticised so not recyclable. A big university with many students, many buildings, many car parks, many visitors every day, many amended lists and many unrecyclable pieces of plasticised paper.

The whole cost – staff, time, environmental, is hidden waste! I cannot estimate the cost without some meaningless guess and sums. You dear Readers are smart enough to get the point (or make your own guesses!)

Now, I have no issue with the University managing its parking spaces. But, how much easier, cheaper would it be if, either UP or JB could log on to a Parking App and book a parking space (verified by UP via a tick box), insert time, duration and, importantly, registration number to the app. The app could send an electronic record to the parking attendant who, on their rounds, could verify that any cars parked were listed.

No email chains, no paper, minimal time for UP and JB, no time at all for the Receptionist who could focus on other duties and responsibilities, money, time and non-recyclable materials would be saved. The only loss would be exercise for JB!

Now, think about how many other apparently sane, sensible and practical improvements could be made just by recognising the Hidden Waste.

Such a system labours under a delusion of efficiency while actually being endemically wasteful of the time and energy of those who use it and is by no means restricted to public services. Governments have pursued narrowly defined efficiency (usually realised as cuts) in public service organisations over many years. This has been pursued from privatisation and outsourcing to mergers and partnerships of public service organisations, centralisation in 'centres of excellence', aggregation of services in shared services and control centres, creation of arms-length 'executive agencies', closure of local health and other public facilities and consequent (but perhaps not commensurate) increases in the size of 'major' or 'regional' hospitals, health centres, schools. Mazzucato (2018) challenges this approach saying 'a proper look at the real cost savings that such outsourcing provides – especially taking into account the lack of 'quality control' and absurd costs that ensue – is almost never carried out'.

The corollary to this process of aggregation has been to increase both the physical and psychological distance between the population served and the service location. Rather than improving the efficiency of the system it has, like self-service tills in stores or the shift to self-completion of tax returns, simply displaced a greater part of the cost to the customer, something Ohno challenges saying 'The question is whether or not the product is of value to the buyer. If a high price is set because of the manufacturer's cost, consumers will simply turn away'. 'Provider' and 'citizen' can substitute for manufacturer and consumer in that last sentence and learn something of importance for the provision of efficient public services. There is psychological and physiological stress imposed on the service user who has to undertake the 'work' of travelling to access a service. This is a real challenge for those of limited financial means with the effect of inhibiting their access to the service and increasing the systemic cost of service delivery BUT applying that cost to the service user. There is an impression of a lack of care for the individual, who may not be able to afford to access the service and community, and there is a load imposed on family members or others to support them.

The absence of a police or fire station, hospital or school in any given location generates a gap between the service people believe they are paying for and the service they perceive they are receiving. Whether or not a police officer on the street makes any actual difference to the level of crime, there is nonetheless a sense of reassurance to the public from their presence just as there is from the availability of a doctor. In comprehending the 'value' of public services as opposed to their 'cost' the psychological dimension needs to be included along with a good understanding of the benefits of prevention as much as cure. Taguchi (1987) proposes that our definition of financial cost should include 'the total cost imparted to society from the moment the product is shipped'. If we embrace this in our thinking, which has profound consequences, and recognise the multiple dimensions to cost of time, money, customer and environment, then it is clear that any definition of efficiency must include the cost to society. In calculating the cost and value of a service, we must treat users or consumers as part of the system rather than external to it; including their costs and those of their supporters for travel, lost earnings, parking, perhaps accommodation will dramatically change the business case. The 'total cost imparted to society' in pursuit of user-friendly, citizen supportive, environmentally sustainable services must be used as a new way of comprehending public service efficiency.

Systemic effectiveness

Effectiveness is the measure of the degree to which a system achieves its intended outcomes and those are a function of its purpose. In order to understand effectiveness, we must be clear about what we intend to achieve.

There are a number of possible combinations arising from any system, it can be:

Effective AND efficient;

Effective NOT efficient;

Efficient NOT effective;

Neither efficient NOR effective.

It does not matter how cheap any activity is or how much we reduce its costs, if it does not contribute towards the desired outcome, it is all waste. Doing the wrong thing can never be efficient, doing the wrong thing better is not an improvement to celebrate.

To design effective and intelligent public services, there are two things with which we need to be concerned. First is to be utterly clear about the purpose to be fulfilled, second is to be utterly clear about what constitutes the system we are considering. We need to know where its boundaries lie and, more importantly, to be able to explain and justify them. We have already talked about the criticality of clarity of purpose in earlier chapters, here we need to consider system boundaries.

Ulrich (1983) is concerned with the idea that the meaning and validity of judgements and decisions about matters which affect the population is dependent upon how, where and why we draw boundaries to systems. Ideas of effectiveness and efficiency mean boundaries become of critical importance in our decision-making as objectives and outcomes falling beyond the boundary are not considered in the arguments, only those falling inside. It is a matter of considerable importance that boundaries are well-judged, their location (physical, digital or behavioural) understood and accepted, and that their influence not just on the decisions we DO make but on the decisions we CAN make are understood. When the system boundaries are not well chosen, then the outcome sought cannot be delivered, it cannot be systemically effective. A small example may help us here.

The E-prescription: A patient

THEN

A patient receiving continuing healthcare support emailed a prescription request to the local health centre collecting it in person 3 days later. The patient took the prescription to the nearest pharmacy, waited for it to be filled and took it home. When reauthorisation was required appropriate tests were carried out at the health centre, the prescription was reauthorized and the process continued as before.

NOW

When a prescription is filled by the (now) nominated pharmacist; they request the prescription electronically from the health centre and the patient collects the products from the pharmacist.

The pharmacist tells the patient when reauthorisation is required; the patient organises relevant tests but does not receive confirmation of the reauthorisation.

When the patient needs the next prescription filled, they go to the pharmacist to discover they have not yet received the reauthorisation either so have not requested it.

The patient then goes to the health centre where the receptionist confirms the prescription has been re-authorised and forwards the authorisation to the pharmacist.

The patient must then return to the pharmacist for a second time to collect the filled script.

Sadly, in the particular instance that inspired this tale, the second visit to the pharmacist was unsuccessful, the prescription was not there. The patient had to revisit the health centre, re-request the prescription and telephone the pharmacist the following day to verify it was received and available.

The patient no longer has control of the process. If the professionals in the chain do not understand the process, or do not use it properly the patient spends a lot more time on ensuring they receive their scripts when they need them.

Health service 1 – Patient 0

Perhaps it is worth noting that we only apply this process to sick people!

Here we can see, setting aside poor process and information systems design and the additional work (waste) generated, that the 'system' excludes the patient; they are outside its boundary. The 'improvement' has been designed around the healthcare professionals, the cost to or impact on the patient ignored but the citizen is at the heart of the nation, they are at the core of the whole, how can they be so excluded? Star (1991) shows how critical it is that a system designed for a mass-market must be designed to deal with individual needs and nuances, surely an advantage of the digital age.

In (re)designing our systems of public services, we must place the service user in the system; rather than being 'just' the customer, the service user is the point of the system and its beneficiary. When we discuss system effectiveness and efficiency, we must measure or evaluate the impact of the system on the customer. We must ask whether the system was effective, whether purpose was fulfilled, outcome achieved; we need to consider whether it was efficient when we also take account of the cost, time and carbon impact on the customer. Let us deal with a worked healthcare example. All the numbers are estimates.

Delusions of efficiency: Dr. John Beckford

As is commonly the case a major hospital provides a full range of services to patients with emergency, elective and chronic needs through both in-patient and out-patient services. The demand for increased efficiency in the use of expensive equipment, highly-trained clinical staff and expensive buildings has seen an inexorable transfer of more and more services to this hospital with a commensurate decline in services provided at community and cottage hospitals and at local health centres. The business cases have been stark. The cost to the health service of treating each individual patient falls substantially when they attend dedicated facilities for treatments such as renal dialysis, radiotherapy or chemotherapy. This happens because utilisation of machines, staff and equipment increases. The relatively fixed costs (staff, premises, equipment) to the service is spread across a greater number of patients while the increases in marginal cost associated with additional patient volume are more than offset by the savings in staff and equipment at local facilities. So, job done? Argument over? Not really. The cost considered only extends to the service itself, the business case is internally focused.

What happens to the argument when we take account of the cost to service users and their supporters? I am going to build this argument around reasonably densely populated Southern England where the distance between major population centres probably averages around 20 miles. If the argument holds here it may also hold for larger, less densely populated locations. The total population is roughly split with 33% in the same town as the hospital, 66% spread evenly across the smaller population centres (I know this is not precise but I did look at the relevant population splits for southern England and it is good enough). Diseases and disorders requiring frequent hospital visits (those suggested above) are spread proportionately to the population. So, 66% of those requiring such visits are required to travel to the hospital to receive treatment and to return home, an average 40-mile round trip. Given the distance and an equal split between private and public transport (or some combination thereof) it is reasonable to assume that each patient is now travelling an hour or so each way to receive treatment. Remember these people are unwell, many will require support, perhaps a non-emergency ambulance, a volunteer hospital car, a taxi a partner, husband, wife or other relative to drive them to and fro. For each centralised service, several hundred (at least) patients every day are required to undertake a two-hour return journey, commonly supported by another person. That journey will generate additional emissions from the transport system, probably lead to loss of earnings (patient and supporter) and some additional expenditure (coffee, parking). Suddenly the efficiency gain claimed by the service is looking fragile. The total cost of the system (its productivity plus its waste) is likely higher than before but the excess is borne by the user not the supplier.

If we consider the problem systemically, it is likely that the overall system efficiency would be higher if more services were delivered more locally (eliminating or substantially reducing the journey times and emissions) AND the impact on earnings of partners and supporters was taken into account. In this case the service has boosted its internal efficiency NOT by improving its process to reduce costs but by exporting part of the total cost to the service user. This is something that can also regularly be observed in commercial organisations. A supermarket makes its customers do the work of collecting goods from shelves rather than serving them, self-check in and baggage handling at airports displaces time and cost to the traveller because the same amount of work is being done in total, just not by airline employees. The total system cost often increases and more of it is borne by the customer. I am sure you can provide your own examples.

Ahh! I hear you cry, what about clinical outcomes, is that not part of the system? Does this apply to everything? The clinical outcome is the ultimate measure of system effectiveness so it is critical to the whole. However, if the system is not effective it cannot be efficient! The question is difficult to answer as a generality. It will depend on a whole range of other factors, in particular the extent to which the expertise of the clinician is the critical factor in achieving the outcome. So, it may be that for the three cases suggested previously (chemotherapy, radiotherapy and renal dialysis) which, post diagnosis and determination of treatment protocol, are process biased, that the most effective and systemically efficient service would be provided locally, even if the cost to the provider was higher. However, for, treatments such as heart or brain surgery, the clinical outcome is skills biased, depending much more highly on the skills of the relevant clinician(s); the most effective and systemically efficient service would be provided in a specialist centre.

The challenge is to deal with each of these cases adopting a systemic financial, clinical and emissions model, a methodology, that includes ALL of the costs borne by the service itself and its users and their supporters and to recognise the particular and specific set of circumstances that surround each community. The likely outcome would be to reinforce and enhance local services through small hospitals, residential care facilities and increased capability at GP surgeries. Localisation would be systemically more effective.

If we are going to improve systemic effectiveness and efficiency, we need to define the outcomes that are to be achieved, and be conscious in defining boundaries that include the service user (in every respect) and take account of multiple outcomes – for customers, cost and carbon. We must recognise that the system definition, purpose and boundaries matter because they also define what we can and will use as metrics and how we can and will understand performance. We can then optimise the design and distribution of services to optimise the mix of local, regional and national delivery.

Organising for citizen outcomes

No nation can consider itself intelligent if its citizens are denied adequate food, housing, healthcare, education and employment. It should be considered offensive in a wealthy country, where there is a surplus of everything, that these things are not universally achievable even though they are available. However, it would be neither desirable nor feasible to offer a solution based on an alternative 'one size fits all' replacement for the current arrangements, it really is more difficult than that. It is possible to suggest some principles as a stimulus to the national discussion that is really needed:

> Success should be understood in terms of the outcome not the inputs;
> Funding should attach to the service user not the service provider;
> Services should be systemic and integrated not functional;
> Delivery should be via the most effective channel;
> Services should be as local as is possible.

Service processes must be designed backwards from the desired outcomes considering the most appropriate means and mode for effective and efficient delivery of each service. This requires a shift to a customer focus while inhibiting asystemic and pathologically autopoietic centralising behaviours. These services must exploit the opportunities made available by digital technology, must integrate services so that they deal with first-hand needs delivered locally. Only those things which cannot be delivered locally may be regionalised or centralised, and the tension between the parts and the centre needs to be managed recognising the legitimacy of a national policy adapted to local needs.

The required outcomes for each systemic element of the social infrastructure need to be agreed and the funds set aside in order to achieve them; without clarity of required outcome and an optimised process no meaningful assertion can be made about the requisite level of resources. All alternative business models from state provision through nationalised operators, privatised organisations or contracts, charities, trusts and community interest companies are available, not on a basis of political preference but from understanding what model is most effective for the service user. An effective regulatory system will help ensure that the desired balance of interests is preserved regardless of business model and ownership. In Estonia, for example, the citizens of Tallinn[10] in 2013 chose to provide free public transport to all residents after recognising that the bulk of the costs were already met from public funds. Meanwhile the franchised privatisation of the railways in the UK has reverted to a model that looks a lot like nationalisation with revenue and cost risk reverting, whether temporarily or permanently, to government.

None of this is easy to resolve, no answer can be absolutely right any more than any answer can be absolutely wrong. Each will have more or less desirable attributes. If though we start with a principle of Intelligent Organisation, then we should design with both citizen control and citizen outcome in mind. The following case study shows an attempt to move beyond functional, discipline-based arrangements and develop an outcome focus.

MADE: Sustainable change in the public sector: Professor Peter Kawalek

The challenge of organizational change and new technology is typically met by bringing in large-scale, external expertise from the private sector to the public sector. Such projects can be expensive and disruptive. Failure rates are high. The Multi-Agency Data Exchange (MADE) in Lancashire exemplifies an alternative approach based on decentralized, local decision-making with high autonomy. The aim was to achieve sustainable change at low cost. Nearly 20 years since its inception, despite funding crises in the UK public sector, MADE still operates successfully and proves its worth in the reporting and planning functions of Lancashire. Originally, MADE was one of a suite of initiatives undertaken in the UK. It has outlived other, more expensive initiatives and continues to function successfully despite its much lower project spend.

The Crime and Disorder Act of 1998 provided for a process of audits across local agencies in a given area. The concept was that partners could share information in order to come up with combined approaches to community safety. In such an approach, many agencies might have key insights and data that could be shared in the development of community plans. The police service, the council, the health service, probation, fire services, drug rehabilitation and action teams; all might have some insight into issues of community safety. In order to share data among such partners, agreements and new technology were needed and organizational processes needed to be developed to bring combined knowledge to decision making and planning.

Lancashire is a county in the north-west of England, covering a geography north of the cities of Liverpool and Manchester, and south of the English Lake District. It includes the urban areas of Preston, Lancaster, Burnley, Blackburn and Blackpool; areas rich in industrial and social history but also characterised by industrial decline and social issues. The administrative structure is complex between district councils, the county council and unitary authorities.

MADE was formed in early 2001 as a central repository of data and analysis operating under the Crime and Disorder Act 1998. Its aims were the same as other initiatives in other localities. In order to improve community safety and to curb crime, the act stipulated that various agencies should work collaboratively at the local government level. As time has gone on since this inception point, the original legislation proved to be just a starting point. There have been new opportunities and pressures for data-sharing, both technological and organizational. These, in turn, have led to an increasingly demanding legal framework.

Looking back over her involvement in the project over nearly two decades, principal Analyst Melanie Greenslade acknowledged 'The requirement to share data has been strengthened in subsequent legislation'.

Key decisions at the outset

It was decided that MADE would be developed in-house, by team members from Lancashire Council and Lancashire Constabulary, with systematic engagement from the other public agencies. Funding was given by these various agencies (county council, unitary council, district councils, the constabulary, fire, National Health service and probation services) in order to support their compliance with the Crime and Disorder Act. The only external expertise brought in came from Manchester and Salford universities in the form of advice given by two academics. These academics had prior experience of public-sector change projects in Salford City Council (Kawalek, 2007). They were able to reinforce and support decisions taken by leadership in Lancashire Council and Constabulary that this project should be led at the local level with high autonomy. There would be high visibility to the partners and to the organizational hierarchies, but decisions were taken locally by the officers leading the project.

Meetings among partners were undertaken in various public buildings across the county. The aim was to consult and inform. Partners were also asked to sign-up to data-sharing protocols. This was potentially a difficult topic, as public agencies are known for cautious interpretation of data protection legislation. Working with legal advice from Lancashire Council, the team were able to identify simple rules around the taking out of personal identifiers in the data, and how it would be published using post-code and geo-location markers. This advice helped the different agencies understand how they could proceed with data sharing and avoided uncertainty over the interpretation of legislation.

The central repository of data required hardware, software and human resource investment (Wastell et al., 2004). Emphasising a low-cost and tactical approach initially summary data of MADE partners was combined into an Excel spreadsheet that was heavily customised to allow reporting of different data sets (e.g. crime and disorder 'hotspots' across different problem types; ward-level profiles of crime data). The use of this Excel spreadsheet lasted longer than an initial prototype phase, becoming widely utilized by different partners for the preparation of audits and other reports. Behind it was an Access database into which data released from partners was fed before the publishable version was made available in Excel. Compared to other projects in other parts of the country, this approach was noteworthy for its simplicity. Other projects had made significant investments in sophisticated Geographical Information Systems (GIS).

There were potential functional advantages in these GIS systems but their procurement and set-up costs were much higher and they required much more training of users. It followed that MADE was able to achieve uptake and use of its system much more quickly and widely than projects in other parts of the country. This wider use encouraged confidence among the agencies in Lancashire as well as helping to further embed its decentralized ethos. The MADE team acted as a hub among the different partners who would take receipt of new versions of the spreadsheet as well as sharing problems and ideas among themselves. A review of all national projects undertaken under the Crime and Disorder Act confirmed this. MADE had the simplest solution but the greatest buy-in. It was also spending the least money. As the first full-time officers were appointed to MADE, the spreadsheet was augmented by a new Oracle based system, and then latterly further enhanced through Microsoft Power BI. Although data-sharing through reports remains a key function of MADE, its more sophisticated technological infrastructure meant that it was increasingly adept in handling requests for analysis and data from partner agencies.

Why did MADE work?

Today MADE remains operational. It is physically located within Lancashire Council and it continues to work with public sector partners across the geography of Lancashire. The financial environment of the public sector has been very difficult since the financial crisis of 2007/8 and then the subsequent cuts to public expenditure from 2010. It follows from this that the continued funding of MADE throughout this period is testimony to its worth.

MADE combines Oracle, Microsoft BI and Ordnance Survey GIS mapping information. There is a web of relations across the council and other partners so that the MADE team are not only able to share expertise but also to receive expertise and information. There are discussions about its extension into Big Data. This would be natural, given that the MADE team are expert in taking data from multiple sources.

The way in which the MADE project was developed prioritised learning and adjustment as the work was done. The original project was undertaken at a time when data sharing across agencies was uncommon. There were technical and legal barriers. The MADE project was then organised as a problem-solving initiative that was not structured through a rigid project plan. Instead it was understood as 'situated innovation' (Wastell, 2006). Officers were able to collaborate together, to take advice (e.g. from lawyers or from academics), and to work out solutions to problems themselves. They were not kept to a bureaucratic timetable nor to a rigid structure by senior management. Equally important, the project was not beholden to a powerful external consultancy whose financial charges would mandate a more structured, less flexible approach to developing the learning required. The project was decentralized, localised and learning was shared. A clear sense of purpose developed. Reviewing the project in 2019, Peter Langmead-Jones, Greater Manchester Police, one of the founders of the original project stated, 'We were very clear about purpose. We made some good choices very early on. … We understood what it was for. [In the Crime and Disorder Act of 1998] there was a requirement to do a strategic assessment every year … so one of the main things that MADE was intended for is to facilitate assessment. That gives it a core purpose. It helps partners to conduct the assessment and then to monitor the plans that were put in place to be able to consolidate action upon that assessment. We were really clear about what it was for.'

This case study highlights three major insights. First is the clarity around what was to be achieved, the sense of purpose and ownership by the participants. Second is the conscious localisation of both problem and solution and the close working to overcome challenges. Third is the designed in adaptiveness of the whole project, it is that which has enabled its survival over so many years as it has been able to maintain its relevance to the changing circumstances.

Prevention or cure: Value enabling or value creating

Some aspects of service provision can be thought of as being either preventative, value enabling and future oriented or curative, value generating (or loss reducing) and present oriented. Preventative activity is anticipatory, assisting in the fulfilment of hopes and aspirations. Based on the idea of feedforward information, it anticipates opportunities and challenges and delivers through processes which are essentially educational. Whether it is health, employment, basic, technical or professional education, the point of such services is to maximise the life opportunity of the citizen.

We can consider this in particular in relation to education beyond the statutory requirement. The UK currently has a higher education system in which education is paid for, ostensibly by the student, through a combination of study fees and rents for accommodation and subsistence. Funded by most through a system of loans, the student repays the loan over a subsequent 30-year period through salary deduction. The impact of this is first to impose a significant cost on all students, second to deter at least some capable students from participation in education from which they and wider society might benefit. How can we be sure that a student is participating with fully informed consent? How can we be sure it is valuable for the student and society? A similar system exists in the USA. While the system in one way means that further and higher education can be available for all, it has a number of challenges. Financially disadvantaged or cautious individuals will be deterred from applying in which case the system acts to reinforce existing social positions and reduces mobility, an inequitable outcome. It imparts all of the risk of participation to the student and none to the providing institution, an inequitable outcome. In any system where the service provider has no risk and the beneficiary has no recourse, it is reasonable to assert that someone, somewhere is not receiving the benefit they should, an inequitable outcome.

The ability to charge for services and not be meaningfully accountable for the quality of the outcomes incentivises any organisation to maximise revenue while minimising service provision, even if that is not their intent. The risk for universities is that some students attend who will not benefit from the experience, some will attend but the educational benefit (usually expressed in terms of increased future earnings) will not match the costs incurred (by themselves or wider society). The risk for an intelligent nation is that some students who would benefit will not attend. To create the most opportunity laden future, any person capable of benefitting from advanced education must have access to it and the providing institutions must be held to account by the student and society for the quality of what is provided. This may mean setting and reaffirming entry standards and requirements (though not necessarily through a traditional qualification route), because that allows appropriate selection, while establishing effective external review of delivery standards and genuine competition on quality and cost grounds between alternative providers. The crucial factor here is that those most likely to need help and support with prevention of future issues are also those least likely to be equipped to access them. The systems are complex, the rules difficult to comprehend, the staff difficult to access, they are designed (it seems) to minimise expenditure (or at least control it within a given budget) rather than to deliver the desired outcome. Change is needed.

The second approach is based on the idea of feedback information; its focus is curative, responsive and reactive. Such services are delivered through approaches aimed at improving the current position. Many citizens in need of support are experiencing multiple challenges, so an Intelligent Nation must provide useful responses to those challenges, as far as possible, through a single intervention with a nominated organisation (perhaps the first contact) taking responsibility for arranging the whole of provision. However, the budget for the service must belong to the citizen who is able to draw on it within whatever limits and rules are established equally for all. It cannot be acceptable that a citizen is denied a service because the particular institution or service provider they encounter has spent its budget. Any public service that places the risk on the individual and provides no recourse generates an inequitable outcome.

A patient presenting at an emergency department with an immediate clinical need may also be found to be malnourished, living in poor conditions, homeless or to have a mental illness. Clinicians treating that patient will know that however good the treatment, the patient once discharged will almost certainly re-present in a short time unless action is taken to address the other conditions (which may or may not be causative but certainly inhibit effective treatment). Rather than referring the patient to another agency, an effective treatment protocol within the institution must incorporate the requirement to address those other needs (provided the citizen will let them). Similarly, people arrested are often found to be struggling with mental health, substance abuse and other life issues so an effective policing response is not simply that of arrest, detention and prosecution but also one of prevention, tackling the challenge of inhibiting future offences. The capability to do these things needs to be embedded within the relevant processes, not provided as a separate function or by a separate agency.

Financial support will need to be redesigned, so that it is always available AND is directed towards supporting the citizen in the achievement of the desired outcome through the primary provider. The money must be made to follow the service user, not the provider. The entitlement of the individual needs to be explicitly recognised so that needs can be met without the arbitrary biases of functional budgeting and commissioning systems. Providers, regardless of ownership, must report citizen outcomes from their delivery processes alongside cost control with a focus on both prevention and cure, success being defined as the non-recurrence of the identified problem for any individual. This should be arranged at local, regional and national levels with a rigorous methodology for determining systemic efficiency and effectiveness acting as the determinant of levels. Evidence for the value of this approach would take time to develop but The Center on Society and Health at Virginia Commonwealth University[11] asserted that 'Americans with more education live longer, healthier lives than those with fewer years of schooling' continuing that the complex 'links tied closely to income and to the skills and opportunities that people have to lead healthy lives in their communities'. The evidence is out there, we must choose to see it.

Nothing is said here of the technical content of the service. In an Intelligent Nation, it does not matter whether the service is policing, healthcare, education, it must always seek to do the two things, enable desired future outcomes and ameliorate current outcomes where they do not meet the desires of the customer/citizen. Provision of funding should be, must be, integral to these processes as a whole not provided by a different agency or require the citizen to demonstrate the need to another party.

Efficiency of the whole system will be achieved when the most cost-effective means of delivery is used whether that be virtual, digitally enabled or first hand. All predominantly rule-based services which are process driven and involve the collection of revenues and distribution of benefits must be embedded in digital systems that provide real-time or near real-time responses. The massive advantage of digital working is that with a given set of rules individually tailored packages can be provided for each citizen; a mass customisation of public services, all focused on delivering the desired outcome. There can be no excuse for delay and, where rules cannot be embedded in a digital system, the rules must be simplified rather than the system made more complex.

Digitally enabled services require some element of human interaction, and it is fatuous to believe that every process can be reduced to a series of yes/no decisions. Digitally enabled services will, like citizens themselves, have a local bias. Location, place-based services, can provide both the anchor for the individual and the basis of revenue collection and benefit distribution. Digitally enabled services may include advisory services, some aspects of education, provision of some justice services, offender education and training, provision of some aspects of medical care.

Everybody has to be somewhere and first-hand services will be those where human interaction is critical to the provision of the service which may include a range of activities from personal care (washing, feeding, clinical treatment, physical therapy), extended personal interactions and consultations, physical interventions, education, medical care and so on.

A necessary part of a decentralised approach is to establish a local revenue base more responsive to local needs. That leaves to central government the revenue and benefit challenge of 'levelling up' nationally and for progression of national policies of defence, international engagement and encouraging national education programmes on issues such as road safety or smoking as was done in Vietnam[12].

Each person has fundamental and social infrastructure that enables their lives and their local society, the networks in which they reside. They have freedom and responsibility within that layer to create the society they desire and can make their own arrangements for the provision of desired services. The requirement for maximum appropriate autonomy demands that the state delivers nationally those things which can only be delivered nationally with all else distributed as far as possible.

An outline architecture is proposed in Figure 4.2. which can be adopted to maintain the principle of subsidiarity by maximising competences at the lowest level, that of the individual, and achieve closure through the democratic process. Here the individual citizen delegates competences upwards to the local, regional and national levels of government to act on their behalf, periodically controlling this through the electoral process. National government deals only with national matters then creates policy which is adapted to local needs as it progresses through levels of government. Service delivery needs to be aligned with this and it is clear that national government must be constrained to deliver only those things for which it is granted competence. Delivery of other services would be regionalised and localised. This requires an inversion of current common practice, to ask not what can be delegated from the centre but what cannot be delivered locally taking account of expertise, demand/availability or total system cost. In a highly localised system of governance, it is important that each politician only hold office at one level in the system and that there is real, agreed, clarity around the limits to authority for each level. Power should only be delegated from the citizen to the state in very controlled amounts.

Summary: Living with complexity

In Table 4.1, those structural ideas for developing intelligent social infrastructure are summarised in an indicative chart, a starter for debating the geographically and politically hierarchical distribution of public services and the most appropriate mechanism for their provision. It is not for any individual to say 'do it this way' but rather to ask, 'is this a useful way of thinking about it'?

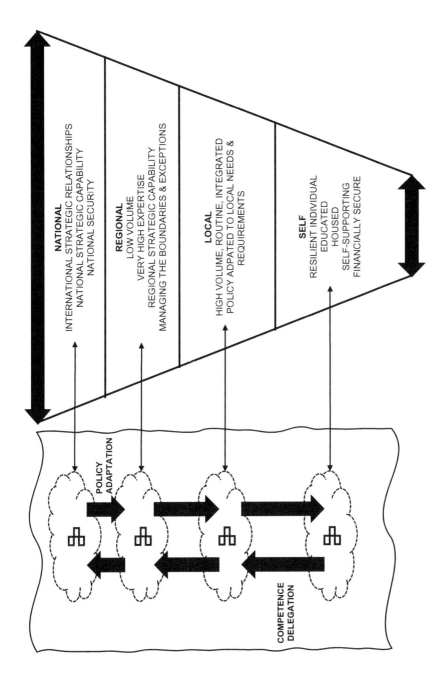

NATIONAL
INTERNATIONAL STRATEGIC RELATIONSHIPS
NATIONAL STRATEGIC CAPABILITY
NATIONAL SECURITY

REGIONAL
LOW VOLUME
VERY HIGH EXPERTISE
REGIONAL STRATEGIC CAPABILITY
MANAGING THE BOUNDARIES & EXCEPTIONS

LOCAL
HIGH VOLUME, ROUTINE, INTEGRATED
POLICY ADPATED TO LOCAL NEEDS &
REQUIREMENTS

SELF
RESILIENT INDIVIDUAL
EDUCATED
HOUSED
SELF-SUPPORTING
FINANCIALLY SECURE

POLICY
ADAPTATION

COMPETENCE
DELEGATION

FIGURE 4.2 Subsidiarity in action

TABLE 4.1 Distributing public services

	Digital	*Digitally-enabled*	*First hand*
National	• Taxation for National Services • Redistributive Policies • Policing, e.g. Cyber, CSE • Regulation of Commerce & Utilities	• Defence, e.g. Counter-terrorism • Policing, e.g. illegal narcotic importation • Tertiary Academic Education • Strategic Business & Supply Chains • National Health Preventative & Education	• Defence • National Infrastructure • Strategic Transport
Regional	• Taxation for Regional Services	• Policing, e.g. Illegal Narcotic Distribution and Production • National Infrastructure • Tertiary Professional and Technical Education (e.g. online learning)	• Regional Infrastructure • Regional Transport • Specialist Healthcare
Local	• Taxation for Local Services • Civil Administration • Revenues and Benefits • Fines & Penalties	• Special Educational Needs • Housing & Homelessness • Primary & Secondary Education • GP Healthcare, Social Care • Acute	• Policing, e.g. neighbourhood, roads, local narcotic distribution • Recycling • Direct health & social care interventions

Adopting the principles outlined here and integrating services is to recognise the lived complexity of contemporary society. The essence of our learning is that the society we end up with is a product of the sub-systems we create and their interactions. In changing one element of one sub-system, we create a perturbation that flows through all of the others. We can neither improve nor neglect one without consequential impact on the others, for good or evil. While the French approach based in areas of responsibility is perhaps more systemic in mindset than those of the UK and USA, each offers a different perspective. Whichever way it is done, we can interpret each of these approaches as recognising a need to preserve the way of life of the country and to do so will require perpetual reinvention, disruption and innovation, not bureaucracy and self-preservation.

To be an Intelligent Nation requires the development, design and building of an adaptive system of citizen centred, public services, geographically distributed through digital, digitally enabled and first-hand delivery. The functional separation both of and between services must be overcome, and the system reflects the outcomes to be achieved by and for the citizens not the inputs provided by the state.

Key points

- Society emerges from the interactions of people with each other and the social and fundamental infrastructures;
- Synthesis of nation and infrastructures needs a legitimate organising mechanism which we call government and its work is governance;
- Social and Fundamental Infrastructure systems coexist in a complex dynamic system but are currently managed and largely owned as functional, independent units;
- Social infrastructure enables services: healthcare, education, civil administration, defence and regulation of commercial organisations (however they may be owned);
- The function of social infrastructure is to enable the well-being of the citizen regardless of ethnicity, gender, sexuality, disability, religion, age, economic situation or other difference;
- Service provision should be about long-term value not short-term cost;
- Services should be localised as far as possible;
- Cost, when calculated, must include the cost imparted to the service user (who must be treated as part of the system) as well as the environmental and social costs;
- Efficiency and effectiveness must be understood from a systemic perspective;
- Services must be redesigned backwards from the desired citizen outcomes and understood as value enabling (future oriented) or value creating (present oriented);
- Services must be designed to use the most cost-effective mode of delivery: digital, digitally enabled, first hand with subsidiarity dominant in determining the level at which each decision is made;
- Power is delegated to the state from the individual.

References

Barrow, C.J., (2006) *Environmental Management for Sustainable Development*, Routledge, London

Beckford, J., (2017) *Quality, A Critical Introduction,* 4th Edition, Routledge, London

Braithwaite, J., (2008) *Regulatory Capitalism*, Edward Elgar Publishing, Cheltenham, UK

Cabinet Office, (2018) *Community Resilience Development Framework*, HM Government, Crown Copyright

Official Journal of the European Union, (2008) *Council Directive 2008/114/EC, On the Identification and Designation of European Critical Infrastructures and the Assessment of the Need to Improve their Protection, Council of the European Union*, pp. 345–375, 23/12/2008

Kawalek, P., 2007. The Bubble Strategy. *International Journal of Public Sector Management* Vol. 20, No. 3, pp. 178–191

Lomborg, B., (2004) *The Skeptical Environmentalist*, Cambridge University Press, Cambridge, UK

Lovelock, J., (1995) *Gaia: A New Look at Life on Earth*, Oxford University Press, Oxford

Lovelock, J., (2019) *Novacene*, Penguin, UK

Mazzucato, M., (2018) *The Entrepreneurial State*, Penguin, London

Ohno, T., (1988) *Toyota Production System*, Productivity Press, New York

Rinaldi, S.M., et al. (2001) Identifying, Understanding and Analysing Critical Infrastructure Interdependencies, *IEEE Control Systems Magazine*, 0272-1708/01, USA

Star, S.L., (1991) Power, Technology and the phenomenology of conventions: on being allergic to onions in *A Sociology of Monsters*, John Law (ed), Routledge, London

Taguchi, G., (1987) *Systems of Experimental Design*, Vols 1 and 2, Unipub/Kraus International Publications, New York

Ulrich, W., (1983) *Critical Heuristics of Social Planning*, Haupt, Berne

Wastell, D., Kawalek, P., Langmead-Jones, P. and Ormerod, R., (2004) Information systems and partnership in multi-agency networks: an action research project in crime reduction. *Information and organization*, 14(3), pp. 189–210

Wastell, D.G., (2006) Information systems and evidence-based policy in multi-agency networks: the micro-politics of situated innovation. *The Journal of Strategic Information Systems*, 15(3), pp. 197–217

Notes

1. https://beckfordconsulting.com/wp-content/uploads/2019/11/Modernising-National-Infrastructure-Draft-2009.pdf 06/04/2020
2. https://www.cpni.gov.uk/critical-national-infrastructure-0 05/03/2020
3. https://www.cisa.gov/critical-infrastructure-sectors 05/02/2020
4. http://www.sgdsn.gouv.fr/uploads/2017/03/plaquette-saiv-anglais.pdf 05/02/2020
5. https://api.parliament.uk/historic-hansard/commons/1828/feb/28/police-of-the-metropolis-and-the-districts-adjoining-thereto 20/06/2020
6. https://assets.publishing.service.gov.uk/government/uploads/system/uploads/attachment_data/file/705347/6.4391_CO_National-Security-Review_web.pdf 20/06/2020
7. https://www.justiceinspectorates.gov.uk/hmicfrs/wp-content/uploads/state-of-policing-2018.pdf 20/06/2020
8. https://www.npcc.police.uk/documents/Policing%20Vision.pdf 20/06/2020

9. https://www2.deloitte.com/content/dam/Deloitte/uk/Documents/public-sector/deloitte-uk-policing-4.0-how-20000-officers-can-transform-uk-policing.pdf 20/06/2020

10. http://www.fleetnews.co.uk/smart-transport/features/how-tallin-provides-free-public-transport-for420-000-people? 19/05/2020

11. https://societyhealth.vcu.edu/work/the-projects/why-education-matters-to-health-exploring-the-causes.html 26/03/2020

12. https://medium.com?'union_TBLH/tobacco-tax-the-most-effective-least-used-tool-in-public-health-997a769f7372 09/01/2020

5

FUNDAMENTAL INFRASTRUCTURE AND UTILITIES

Introduction

Attention can now turn to the provision of fundamental infrastructure for water, waste, information and communication technologies (ICT), transport and energy. These five elements of the fundamental infrastructure, all predominantly value enabling, must be dealt with as a system to address economic, social and environmental opportunity, risk and resilience. Interdependencies and interactions demand this systemic approach which is challenging with a mixed ownership or privately owned, licenced and regulated model. Alternative ownership and investment models including community participation may be more appropriate to the needs of an Intelligent Nation in which the systems must be considered value enabling from the perspective of the whole nation but value generating within their own boundaries. The following case shows the importance of understanding these interactions.

Infrastructure interdependency: Dr. Donya Hajializadeh

A 6-month feasibility study was undertaken to investigate the potential for an integrated decision support system for three infrastructure networks:

- transport in three modes (road, rail and ferry);
- energy;
- drinking water distribution.

The main purposes of the project were to:

- initiate the conversation by considering interdependencies in decision-making and its potential benefits;

- co-create a framework that could have meaningful outcomes for all parties.

The project was conducted in partnership with key members of each participating organisation who understood their system and operation very well and had the authority to incorporate changes at an organisational level.

In comparison to an integrated decision support system 'initiating the conversation' may seem a trivial matter. However, given the risk-averse nature of some of the organisations and fluidity of concepts such as interdependency and resilience, this was the very first instance of having the representatives of these organisations around one table to discuss inherent connections between the networks. The diverse nature of the infrastructures and organisations involved meant that it was of paramount importance to have a common frame of reference and a case study area which would be of interest for all parties involved. A small area in the UK was selected based on past experience of widespread interdependency-induced failures due to extreme weather events.

To provide common grounds for discussions, the conversation started from the shared challenge of climate change. Collectively the decisions were made in two levels:

- immediate responses;
- preventative responses (adaptation for climate change).

These decisions are usually detailed at the individual network level but commonly the interdependencies are missed. For all three infrastructure systems, what is important to whom (the integrated interdependency, criticality and vulnerability assessment) were the most interesting aspects of a potential decision support system.

The discussions started with an overview of each organisation's perception of its own interdependencies. The energy network is generally considered an independent system (with the exception of a high level of dependency on telecommunications). In this network, the transmissions have a high level of redundancy and an extremely low probability of failure. As for the energy distribution system, failures are common however the system is considered to be mainly dependent on telecommunication (not considered in the scope of the study) for operational connections and road network for maintenance purposes.

The nature of the transport system depends on the mode of transport. Roads are considered a fairly independent system at the physical and operational levels, even the electricity required for traffic lights and light poles are provided in isolation and are generally independent from the wider electricity distribution system. However, the impact of failure in other infrastructure systems such as a pipe burst can have a significant knock-on effect on the traffic flow (service). There is also a significant level of dependency on road networks for business continuity of other infrastructure systems. In comparison to roads, the ferry network is considered even more independent although the service flow of roads can have a considerable impact on its operation. In contrast to these networks, rail and drinking water distribution systems have a much more established and well-recognised level of interdependency on electricity, road and telecommunication. The situation becomes even more complicated when considering future changes in each of these systems, for example, the impact of power shortage for charging electric vehicles, affecting flow on a transport network and business continuity in other systems.

Having five different systems, and three sectors with entirely different system configuration and operating regimes make it onerous to capture a comprehensive representation of the inherent connections. With the ultimate purpose of these systems' existence being their vital role in fulfilling human needs, interdependency becomes a societal problem, which makes the definition and formulisation of interdependencies a non-trivial task. The shared ultimate goal, however, offers an opportunity of defining a shared and common performance indicator for all the considered systems, i.e. the number of users receiving service.

In its simplicity, the number of users in service at any given point in time is a meaningful and relatable indicator for all three sectors. It is also convertible into monetary terms because users are entitled to some level of compensation following loss of service. A common performance indicator is also, arguably, transferable to a measure of resilience. It might be used as an appraisal metric to compare costs and savings associated with different mitigation and adaptation strategies such as targeting severity of vulnerabilities and responsive adjustments for optimising, retaining, restoring and transforming the performance of a system.

The connected systems are shown in Figure 5.1 as a series of nodes, links and corresponding service flows. Simulation of the actions and interactions of each individual infrastructure element (nodes and links) was modelled with a view to assess their effects on the system performance as a whole. For this purpose, we defined five main characteristics for each node and link to capture the effect of failure and corresponding recovery on immediate neighbour assets (nodes, links):

- expected performance indicator;
- performance indicator in time;
- failure propagation function;
- recovery initiation time;
- recovery propagation function.

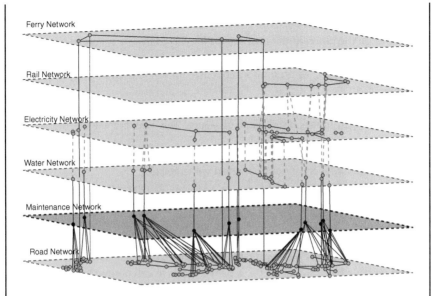

FIGURE 5.1 Interdependence in infrastructure networks

The failure and recovery propagation functions captured the nature of the asset: an asset with a brittle behaviour can experience abrupt and sudden failure/ recovery propagation whereas a more ductile asset can demonstrate a more flexible behaviour in response to failure and recovery.

Having established the definition of interdependencies and common key characteristics for all five infrastructure systems, the next step was to investigate the meaning of these concepts for each sector using a case study. This leads to a further challenge in interdependency research and practice, the lack of detailed information on infrastructure dependencies and interdependencies due to

- lack of availability of such data;
- potential security threats;
- commercial sensitivity;
- lack of incentive to share the data.

With a common understanding that overcoming these fundamental challenges would not be feasible within a 6-month initial study, a decision was made to utilise open access data for the transport network and devise a fictional network for water and energy systems. Despite its simplicity this was a useful exercise as it facilitated the initial aim of initiating the conversation and co-creating a framework. It also meant that we could investigate different levels of interdependency and explore challenges and potential benefits. Rather than focusing on the different threat scenarios for each different system, we looked at the effect of any potential failure in any part of the network for any given magnitude and focused on the consequences for all interdependency-induced failures.

For the first experiment, we looked at all single asset failures and demonstrated the geo-spatial distribution of failure. This was particularly useful to illustrate:

• the hidden interdependency-induced vulnerabilities;
• systemic impact and effect of failure on the network and the users;
• impact and pace of recovery measures.

We then extended the experiment to multi-asset failure scenarios and repeated the investigations. This was important as generally in case of an extreme weather event (either a black swan event or a perfect storm as categorised by Hasan and Foliente, 2015), mutually exclusive failures may occur at different parts of the networks and can disable the entire service provision for different networks.

Figure 5.2 provides a schematic view of the developed framework. As shown, the simplified multi-layered system provides an overview of all five networks and their dependencies and interdependencies. This can be used as a tool to investigate and test the impact of different failure scenarios on the entire multi-layered system. A failure scenario can be defined by selecting one (or more) asset(s) (i.e. nodes/links) and stating the failure time and magnitude for each asset. The first outcome of this exercise is a failure propagation map highlighting the spatial distribution of the scenario (i.e. failure propagation zones). The defined failure

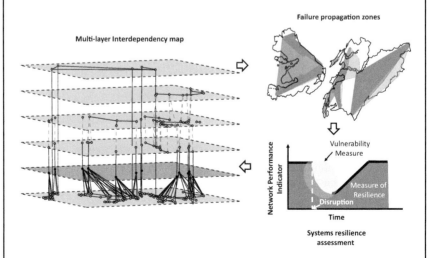

FIGURE 5.2 A framework for exploring interdependency

scenario and corresponding recovery mechanisms can be reflected on the performance indicator of each system with time and the performance indicator of the connected systems as a whole. This provides a measure of system vulnerability and resilience in response to a failure scenario. This can be then converted into the financial implications of service loss. The behaviour of the connected systems for all feasible and plausible failure scenarios can then be used to re-think the structure of the systems and corresponding recovery mechanisms with the ultimate goal of optimising resilience for the multi-layered network (and closing the loop).

These two experiments highlighted how interdependencies expose integrated networks to hidden vulnerabilities. The experiments offered an opportunity to take advantage of these connections through the concept of 'shared intervention' in which the interdependency-induced failures are anticipated, perceived, prioritised and addressed in a collaborative manner. In other words, the assets in each network can be prioritised collectively based on their importance on the asset for the network itself and the interdependent systems. In a scenario where the particular asset is not considered important for the network itself, but its impairment could result in significant loss of service elsewhere, asset owners can discuss the possibility of sharing intervention measures. This could help speeding up the recovery initiation and hence, leading to speedy service restoration in the interdependent network.

Given the simplifications made in the modelling and the fictional nature of the case study, this study was inevitably an inexact exercise, but it provided a useful starting point to a coherent approach by highlighting, and quantifying in a common narrative format, vulnerabilities due to inherent connections. This also provided evidence on how asset owners and managers can turn challenges induced due to independencies to opportunities.

This case study demonstrates the interdependence of assets in networks and the critical need to begin dealing with them as whole systems to reduce the risk of failure and failure propagation.

Functional development of infrastructure networks generates potential for unwitting creation of unrecognised single points of failure in which are embedded the seeds of cascade failures. The tendency to mitigate such failure risks through insurance and contract arrangements is delusory, generating financial compensation for the affected but neither mitigating the risk nor guaranteeing continuity of supply. Such arrangements provide a line of defence for the failed provider ('we mitigated the risk and compensated our customers at the agreed rate') without addressing the risk itself as what they mitigated was the cost of the failure. It may well be that preventing such failures would, in the longer term, be more cost-effective (eradication of lost revenue, reduction in compensation, improved reputation) than the financial risk insurance option so commonly adopted. It is critical for an Intelligent Nation that its fundamental infrastructure is robust and resilient.

Infrastructure interdependency and networks

In 2009, a research project[1] for UK Government under the auspices of Professor Brian Collins undertaken by AEA-Ricardo with this author, set out to undertake the first systemic mapping of the interdependencies (Figure 5.3) of the UK's five fundamental infrastructure elements. Intended to inform the government strategy on infrastructure investment, the work contributed to the Council on Science and Technology Report (2009) report 'An Infrastructure for the 21st Century'. The mapping found that there were no fewer than 67 interdependencies between the elements and that no one element could be considered as wholly independent of the others. The whole system, represented as a network, needs to be treated as a single asset at the level of country. Systemic thinking must be applied to the stewardship of the five elements and the connections between them. Importantly it needs to be recognised that the boundaries which define each supplier (e.g. over 20 water companies in the UK) as a regulated legal entity are not the same as the conceptual system boundaries; in system terms, the sub-system elements are contiguous across dependencies and their functions are interdependent not discrete.

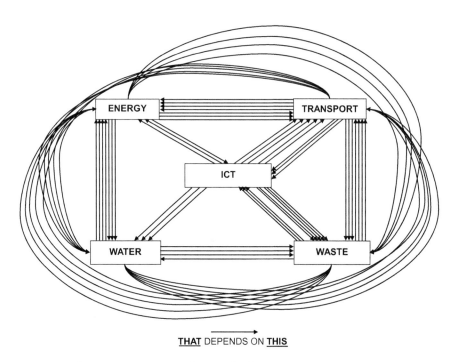

THAT DEPENDS ON THIS

FIGURE 5.3 Systemic interactions of national infrastructure

It was found that there is an absolute underpinning interdependency between energy and ICT which cannot effectively operate without each other while the other three rely on those two for their operation. The research showed that these multiple interdependencies could be stressed or exacerbated by excess load, failure and growth and that there were potential single points of failure risk in the networks with governance of and between the sub-systems fragmented through the ownership models being particularly problematic. There was no ability to systemically manage risk and particular concern arose around the ownership and utilisation of often pro-prietary and commercially sensitive data for decision-making. It was thought that the networks were not resilient to climate change or extreme weather events. It was suggested that there was a need to engage in more effective multi-sectoral planning in pursuit of systemic effectiveness and efficiency, coupled to renewed investment in the underpinning knowledge and skill base. Renewal of national infrastructure was seen as a key need with implications for the policy, planning and regulatory regimes together with a long-term (40–50 years) outline road map.

Few, if any, infrastructure assets are truly independent. Even the solar panels on our roofs (for those of us fortunate enough) are commonly set to require an inbound signal from the grid before they will begin to transmit the electricity they generate. This section will explain how the value-enabling function of any asset in an infrastructure network is subject to and contributes to value-enabling activity.

Figure 5.4 shows an individual asset which is held with an output expectation of a performance (it is expected to do something useful) and some attributes (which I have chosen fairly arbitrarily for the purposes of illustration). Each asset, at the least, is an artefact in a data network concerned with its control and management. We need, as a minimum, to know its:

- Identity: a tag or label that distinguishes THIS asset from any other;
- Location: where it is (including the time of that location, direction of travel and speed if a mobile asset);

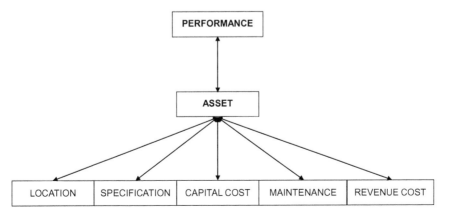

FIGURE 5.4 Individual asset

- Specification: what it is designed to do (output, volume, energy and materials consumption);
- Cost: capital and revenue;
- Performance: outcome (whether or not it does what we intended including condition, reliability, output, cost of operation, degradation rate).

Beyond the local data network through which the asset owner manages performance, the asset is part of two wider networks and subject to multiple forms of dependency.

The first network is of assets owned or operated within the same proprietorship or functional arrangement and on which the performance of the initial asset depends. The second is of assets with different functional arrangements which may be owned or operated within different proprietorship. Dependencies (Figure 5.5) occur on both the inbound and outbound side of our particular asset and into both 'My Network' (the one to which the particular asset belongs) and 'Other Networks' (networks different by function or ownership). These distinctions are important because any asset owner can only fully control and manage assets within their own network. Assets in other networks present dependency risk which must be managed through technical, regulatory and contractual arrangements.

Dependency exists where there is reliance of any sort by one asset on another and is uni-directional; that is, THIS depends on THAT. It may exist within a single network or between networks. Interdependency exists where the reliance is multidirectional; that is, THIS depends on THAT and THAT depends on THIS. A good example of this is the interdependence between energy and ICT systems. The interdependency is such that it may no longer be appropriate to regard them as different networks but rather one, somewhat complex network, a system. The interdependencies may have multiple dimensions; they may be purely functional as outlined above but may also be financial, consumer, geo-physical, weather (short term), climate (long term), they may be operational or concerned with inter-operability, that is, the two assets may need to share language or an

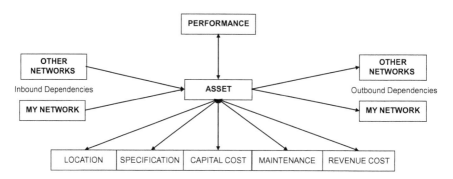

FIGURE 5.5 Asset embedded in a network

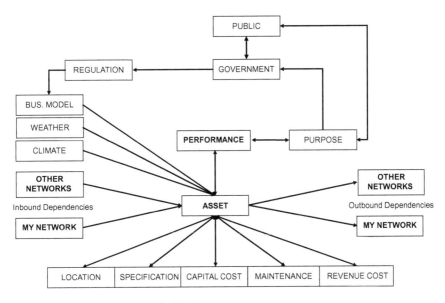

FIGURE 5.6   Asset network embedded in a country

operating system, even something as relatively simple as a plug or socket for con-nectivity. Each additional increase in connectivity increases the complexity of the network rendering it both vulnerable and resilient depending on how well the interdependencies, failure propagation and the risks are understood and man-aged. Network complexity increases in a non-linear manner as a function of the inter-dependencies.

In Figure 5.6 thinking needs to move beyond the fundamental infrastructure network (which now includes weather and climate) to embrace the wider context in which the network of networks exists. Here asset performance is considered a function of fulfilment of a given purpose. Infrastructure provision is regulated, so its purpose is not simply a property prescribed by an owner but a product of a con-versation between the public (which may include the owners) and the government, which generates a regulated business model. That means there is another layer of interdependence, that of infrastructure network economic interdependency. This exists where the operational or investment expenditure is coupled not just to the performance of the particular asset or its network, but to the whole complex set of interdependencies in which change in the performance of one asset affects the performance of another (a change in demand) delivering cost or benefit to that asset or network to which it is then obliged to respond.

It is simply no longer possible to manage or regulate one of these infrastructure networks while being blind to the implications for others. The following case study develops one view of systemic interdependency to help explore the nature of this complex adaptive system.

Resilient infrastructure systems: Dr. Tom Dolan

> Any country that fails to prioritise the systemic resilience of its national system of infrastructure networks (SIN) will regret it: 'Maybe not today, maybe not tomorrow, but soon'.
>
> (Casablanca, adapted)

All aspects of modern societies, including quality of life, social cohesion, economic prosperity and productivity are emergent outcomes enabled either directly or indirectly by a System of Infrastructure Networks (SIN) (Figure 5.7) which has a Sub-System of Economic Infrastructure Networks (EIN) at its core. It produces infrastructure assets and services (IP&S) to power, heat, cool, hydrate, connect, mobilise and sanitise the society it serves; and to enable the movement of food, people, goods, services and ideas within and between societies. It makes possible the operation of social infrastructure facilities (SIF) and provision of social infrastructure services (SIS). The SIN catalyses societal and economic multiplier effects by enabling a range of social and economic activity (IEA) that simply could not occur in its absence and facilitates long term, sustainable, equitable, affordable realisation of the societally beneficial infrastructure enabled outcomes (IEO). The purpose of a SIN is to enable the IEO expected by the citizens and society it serves. The SIN is a critical enabler of national prosperity.

A SIN cannot effectively fulfil its purpose unless it is systemically resilient. This is because a SIN with a low level of systemic resilience will be susceptible to disruption with greater frequency, on a larger scale, with higher intensity and for longer durations (Table 5.1) than one with a higher level. A national SIN with low resilience, will jeopardise the short-term realisation of all other strategic objectives and in the long term any Nation with persistently low resilience is at risk of initiating a downward spiral in which the cumulative impacts of disruptions to the SIN undermine quality of life, reduce productivity and GDP, damage industry and investor confidence, impairing tax revenues and international competitiveness, channelling national resources into responsive expenditure.

Normal operations of the SIN are enabled, constrained and co-evolve in response to the dynamic external environment (DEC) within which it is embedded. Any strategic challenge that disrupts the flow of enabling factors from the DEC, therefore has the potential to disrupt the normal operations of the SIN.

The EIN is at the core of the SIN, enabling it to fulfil its purpose. The EIN is a sub-system, enabled by a predictable flow of Enabling Factors, e.g. supply chain, people, logistics, technology and the whole of the enabling eco-system. It is comprised of:

* Physical infrastructure, Governance structures, management and Regulatory frameworks,

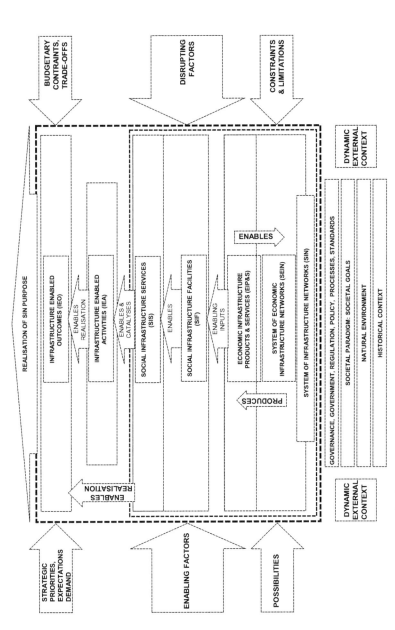

FIGURE 5.7 National infrastructure in context

TABLE 5.1 Overview of disruption dimensions

Dimensions	Description
Frequency of disruption	How often disruptive impacts cascade via interdependent related disruption across the SoI
Scale of disruption	The extent to which disruptive impacts cascade via interdependent related disruption across the SoI
Intensity of disruption	The speed at which disruptive impacts cascade via interdependent related disruption across the SoI
Duration of disruption	The length of time for which the performance of the SoI remains below pre-disruption levels

- Strategic priorities associated with the Economic Infrastructure Networks (EIN)
- Multiple Interdependencies
  - Interdependencies within individual Economic Infrastructure Networks (EIN)
  - Interdependencies between the elements of the EIN
  - Interdependencies between the EIN and the DEC

The normal operation of the EIN both depends upon and produces a predictable flow of infrastructure products and services. Together, the EIN and the flow of IP&S it produces, enable cascade benefits across all levels of Figure 5.7, these include:

- Social Infrastructure Facilities (SIF) and Services (SIS)
- Wider economic and societal activity (IEA)
- Societally beneficial outcomes (IEO)

Therefore, any form of disruption to the normal operations of the EIN that reduces production of one or more IP&S has the potential to initiate interdependence-related disruption (Table 5.2) both within and beyond the EIN.

Systemic resilience overview

Systemic Resilience is a dynamic, emergent and intrinsic characteristic of a system. It encompasses the degree to which any system is able to reduce the frequency, scale, speed, and duration (Table 5.1) of the disruptive impacts (Table 5.2) initiated by Strategic challenges.

Dolan (2017) gives a brief overview of a number of useful conceptual models of resilience, two of which (Table 5.3 and Figure 5.8) are introduced below:

TABLE 5.2 Interdependence-related disruption

Concept (source)	Interpretation
Single point of failure	A disruption to a single system component.
Interdependence-Related Disruption (IRD; Rinaldi et al., 2001)	A disruption to multiple system components that is propagated between system components through interdependence in a system.
Three forms of IRD:	
IRD type 1: Cascade failure	A form of IRD that is initiated by disruption to a single system component and propagates across the system through interdependencies between system components.
IRD type 2: Common cause failure	A form of IRD in which multiple system components are disrupted independently by a common cause, initiating multiple initially independent cascade failures.
IRD type 3: Escalating failure	A form of IRD in which a cascade or common cause failure either occurs, or occurs with greater scale and intensity because the system components disrupted are already operating under stress, or latent vulnerabilities are present in the system.
Normal or system accident (Perrow, 1999)	Terms equivalent to interdependence-related disruption.
Ecosystem accident (Perrow, 1999)	A useful extension to the concept of interdependence-related disruption (IRD) that explicitly acknowledges that IRD can be initiated or propagated by interdependencies between system components and the dynamic external context (DEC) in which a system operates.
High risk system (Perrow, 1999)	A system in which IRD/normal/system accidents are inevitable because components are tightly coupled and interdependent in a complex myriad of ways.
Incertitude (Stirling, 2010)	A term emphasising that four distinct types of incomplete knowledge (risk, uncertainty, ambiguity and ignorance) can be present in a system and each must be managed differently. As system complexity increases, ambiguity or ignorance become the more likely forms of incertitude.

TABLE 5.3 Resilient system capabilities

Ability	Description
The ability to address the actual (respond)	Knowing what to do. How to respond to regular and irregular disruptions and disturbances either by adopting a prepared set of responses or by adjusting normal functioning.
The ability to address the critical (monitor)	Knowing what to look for. How to monitor what is or can become a threat in the near future. The monitoring must cover both events in the environment and the performance of the system.
The ability to address the factual (learn)	Knowing what has happened. How to learn from experience, in particular, how to learn the right lessons from the right experience – successes as well as failures.
The ability to address the potential (anticipate)	Knowing what to expect. How to anticipate developments, threats, and opportunities further into the future, such as potential changes, disruptions, pressures and their consequences.

The resilience construct shown in Figure 5.8 emphasises that resilience is multi-faceted requiring continuous and adaptive strategic management of short-term (people, plans, processes, and procedures) and long-term factors (life cycle asset management, asset design changes, alternative modes of delivery via new technologies).

The intrinsic capabilities of a resilient system (Table 5.3) are emergent characteristics of a highly resilient system. In any complex system, the less developed these capabilities the lower the systemic resilience to disruptive impacts. To develop, sustain and enhance these capabilities requires long term strategic commitment.

Strategic challenges and systemic resilience

National prosperity is enabled by a fit for purpose SIN. Sustaining prosperity requires it to be systemically resilient to the disruptive impacts of any event, decision or trend with disruptive impacts on normal operations of the EIN or IP&S which might generate disruption across it. Exogenous disruptors take effect through one or more of the following mechanisms:

- adversely effecting one or more enabling factors
- causing direct physical damage or disruption to one or more components

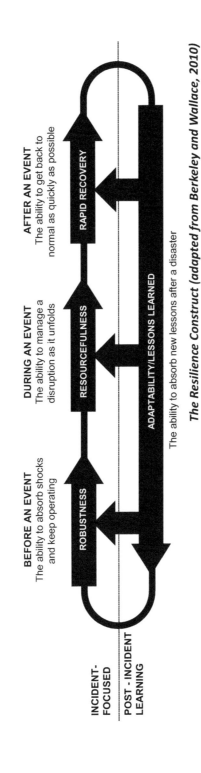

FIGURE 5.8 The resilience construct

- rapid or fluctuating short-term demand change
- increasing the frequency of operation beyond design thresholds with increasing likelihood of an individual component failure

Endogenous disruptors include actions, trends or events in the EIN that:

- Change the likelihood of an initial single point or cascade failure
- Increases the number and criticality of interdependencies
- Alters the relative criticality of individual components
- Results in the system operating outside of design specification for increased periods
- Removes spare capacity
- Optimises the system to inappropriate criteria

Specific examples of Strategic Challenges might include global warming, malicious actions, accidental disruption and numerous other factors inherent in the system itself or the surrounding social, economic, political and physical environment.

Nurturing a systemically resilient SIN

To create and sustain the systemic conditions required for the emergence, growth and sustaining of a systemically resilient National system of infrastructure networks (SIN) requires:

- Policy, Governance, regulatory frameworks, and management/decision making processes for the SIN to be defined for the SIN as a whole and systemically aligned;
- That the Systemic resilience of the SIN as a whole be an explicitly stated strategic priority;
- In-depth systemic understanding of all levels of Figure 5.7;
- A set of long-term collaborative commitments at all stages of the resilience cycle to prioritise actions that develop, sustain and enhance the intrinsic characteristics of a resilient system and to avoid actions that reduce systemic resilience;
- A collaborative, dynamic, multifaceted portfolio of systemically targeted interventions:
  o Collaborative because systemic resilience cannot be achieved by a single organisation in isolation, and interventions need to be targeted at addressing the root causes of systemic vulnerabilities
  o Dynamic because systemic resilience requires continuous action, monitoring review and adaptation to ensure interventions are fit for purpose and sufficient in scope

o Multi-faceted to avoid overdependence on any single intervention or intervention type

o Systemically targeted to address the root causes of low systemic resilience, intervene at the most effective points in the system, with the most effective intervention types, at the most appropriate time.

This case study shows the richness and complexity of interdependence of the fundamental infrastructure. It is neither easy to explore nor explain, but that complexity can no longer be ignored or broken down to functional elements to simplify; in doing so, we deny the nature of the problem being considered.

Asset vulnerability and criticality

If fundamental infrastructure is to fulfil its purposes, then we must not just recognise the rich interdependencies between the many fold assets and interacting networks, but must make those interdependencies an explicit part of how we understand, regulate, invest and utilise them. We must understand how to exploit their utility for the Intelligent Nation as a whole. Figure 5.8 is adapted from work undertaken with Dudley[2] to consider whether modelling of such relationships could be usefully undertaken and whether failure propagation could be comprehended across both individual networks and multiple networks. A database model of UK Infrastructure was created incorporating asset and network information; its application revealed that cycles of asset failure would rapidly propagate across the networks as each failure imposed additional burden on the next connected assets. The model enabled the identification of the particular populations affected by each wave of failure and showed that vulnerable and critical assets in any infrastructure network can be identified and their importance asserted. This importance was not seen to be a function of their size, volume or value of activity but rather a function of the topology of the network, the position and connectedness of each asset within it, that is, the things on which it depends AND the things which depend on it. From that position, it is possible to discern both where mitigation will deliver most benefit to any given population (or all of it) and where additional capability (either more capacity or greater resilience) would deliver most increase in resistance to failure. A resilient value-enabling infrastructure is key to the social infrastructure of an Intelligent Nation, in particular in its ability to generate value.

Figure 5.9 shows how the vulnerability and criticality of each asset in a network can be assessed. The word assessed is chosen carefully, there is work to do in understanding vulnerability and criticality. Asset management and assessment systems such as ISO55000 tend to focus on the management and efficiency (productivity) of individual assets and their risk (or probability) of failure rather than on the integrated performance and failure risk of the system of assets to which they contribute

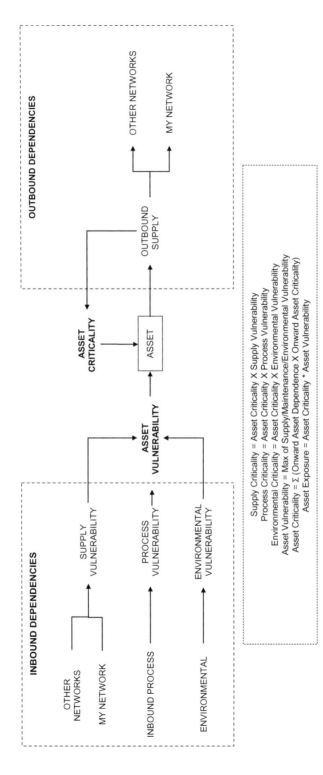

FIGURE 5.9 Asset vulnerability and criticality

(as opposed to the asset management system in which data about them are stored and codified).

Given the state of knowledge, interdependence and systemic risk are not adequately considered. In a dynamic system such as an Intelligent Nation, the performance of any individual asset is at least as much a function of the performance of the assets on which it depends (and which depend on it) as it is on its own internal capability. We can service and maintain any individual asset to minimise its risk of failure or its exposure to environmental risk, while vulnerability to and protection from the performance of other assets must be managed at a system level in the knowledge of connectivity to and reliance on other assets, some of which will be within our control, many of which may not. Looking at Figure 5.9:

> Supply Vulnerability arises because assets in 'My Network' or 'Other Networks' are subject to risk-imparted inadequate maintenance from preceding assets or networks;
>
> Process Vulnerability arises because assets can be stressed by increased or undue load passed to them by other processes or systems, particularly when there is displacement of workload from one to the other. This is visible in transport networks when inclement weather causes disruption at airports and passengers are displaced to train services, or when asset failure on the railway causes loss of services with passengers displaced to bus replacements in both cases with delays and overcrowding. More locally we may see load shift between pumps in a water system or between switches or transformers in an electrical network where increased (or decreased) load in in one network impacts on the performance of another. In traffic management systems (whether road, rail, sea or air) we observe how failure or impairment of a control asset (say traffic signals) generates disruption in flow and then displaces load to other assets within the transport infrastructure. Delayed or failed trains cause delays to trains behind them on the same track or subject to transit through the same node, delays to traffic flows through a failed signal impart delays to other traffic, delays which have a ramifying, somewhat uneven and unpredictable effect on all other connected systems. We need to learn to appreciate, comprehend and manage these system effects across our connected networks of interdependent assets if we are to achieve both efficiency and effectiveness in pursuit of purpose.
>
> Environmental Vulnerability is a function of the physical conditions in which the asset is embedded and the weather (short term) and climate (longer term) impacts upon it. Land may be subject to flood, slip, upheaval, earthquake; the asset itself may be exposed to precipitation, condensation, heat, cold, wind or it may just be placed in a vulnerable position. For example, the nuclear accident at Fukishima in Japan was the consequence of an earthquake generated tsunami against which the defensive walls of the plant were inadequate to prevent inundation. This in turn led to the failure of electrical

generators and as a result flood pumps failed to operate leading to a loss of cooling in the reactor.

Asset Criticality is a function of the dynamically relative importance of any particular asset in the network to those assets and activities downstream of it.

Criticality of any asset in a network is a function of a number of other things. First is the capacity and capability of the asset itself. If it is a major contributor to other processes on its outbound side, then its immediate criticality is very high. Where, for example, this asset is the single source of supply or the single means on which the outbound dependencies rely, then it may be absolutely critical. In a network of interdependent assets, such absolute criticality is less likely but, where found, must be exposed and addressed. In one particular study of a power-generation system, it was discovered that one, highly thermally efficient, power-generation asset relied for its blackstart capability on an adjacent asset which was in course of being closed and dismantled. Second is the contribution to the whole made by any particular asset and the capability of the rest of the network to function with that contribution reduced or impaired; is it a potential single point of failure? The criticality of the asset will be a function of its substitutability and the extent to which the downstream assets rely upon it, and that will change depending on a number of variables such as

the capacity of the whole system, the availability of complementary assets (e.g. other assets generating electricity);

the demand on the system relative to its total capacity;

the variation in demand and the ability of the system to respond;

the availability of alternative means of meeting demand.

Asset criticality will also vary with the functional importance of the particular item to the operation of the other networks. If a traffic light fails at a road junction, then, for the most part, the traffic can continue to flow albeit that flow is likely to be altered, sometimes improved. However, if we assume impairment then, depending on connectivity, topology and activity volume, that impairment is likely to propagate even if the failure itself does not. In other circumstances, 'fail to safe' will have been adopted (e.g. in rail vehicle signalling systems and in nuclear power plants) in which case, the failure of one asset will cease the operation of others. Most of us will be aware of instances of disrupted rail journeys 'caused' by failed signals. The temptation is to think of these things as secondary assets whereas, in practice, they form a key element of the primary system and are as critical to its operation as the permanent way, the vehicles and the power cart on a railway.

Assessment of the vulnerability and criticality of assets in a network is a dynamic problem needing deep comprehension of both structural relationships and performance characteristics as its basis. This comprehension needs to be expressed in a network relationship model which continually compares actual performance with capability at the levels of both individual assets and the network itself. Performance reporting will then allow the generation of a criticality and vulnerability index of the infrastructure network as a whole. For short-term and immediate purposes, that may direct responsive operational interventions to sustain performance. For longer-term strategic and policy purposes, precisely the same index, utilising time-series data will provide the capability to diagnose systemic weaknesses and identify strengths, to simulate the effects of alternative investment strategies and explore the consequences of alternative policy choices and inform decision-making.

The purpose of infrastructure

There can be no single and universal 'right' answer to the challenge of providing fundamental infrastructure. No single or universal business or ownership model can offer a best or universal fit to the different needs of each and every country or every social, economic, environmental or political context. Of particular importance are the political, social and economic maturity of the country in which any particular infrastructural system is being developed, maintained or managed.

The setting of purpose rests in a discussion about what we, the Intelligent Nation, want our fundamental infrastructure for, what is our intention in its creation. Beer (1985) suggests that 'the purpose of a system is what it does' although, we must take account of intent and discuss what the system does (as we experience it) and what we want it to do. In an Intelligent Nation, that is ultimately for the citizens to decide through the democratic processes.

Observing the purpose of the system from the effect that it has allows reflection on whether what is desired is what is achieved. Observers are essentially in four categories: providers, users, regulators and government. These different observers experience different effects and through shared understanding of them, agreement on purpose emerges together with appropriate ownership, business models and performance.

Infrastructure providers, not unreasonably, will align matters to suit their interests, informed by ownership, business and regulatory arrangements. Users will be interested in the outcome the infrastructure enables for them; typically electricity, gas or water are not bought for their own sake but for the work that they do on our behalf and the outcomes that they enable. They provide heat, light, entertainment, communication, hot food, cleanliness perhaps even reduction if not eradication of some levels of disease or disorder. However, if the beneficial effect is outweighed by the cost rendering it unaffordable (utility poverty), then the benefit is moot as it cannot be attained.

Regulators address compliance with the terms, rules and operating licence of the provider. In the UK, the regulators for some are both legally established, for example, water, telecommunications and energy, and mainly concerned with economic compliance, establishing regimes and targets for financial performance. Others such as the UK Office of Road and Rail also have a safety obligation. Beyond these, there are a number of other statutory regulators such as the Health & Safety Executive and the Driver and Vehicle Standards Agency and others which regulate non-economic aspects. In addition, there are voluntary regulatory codes to which many organisations choose to subscribe. In one organisation, during the course of 12 months, some 17 different regulatory inspections by external bodies took place mainly overlapping, always imposing additional compliance cost, sometimes providing contradictory or alternative guidance and recommendations. Clearly, regulation is an area in which there is scope for a different, systemically coherent approach.

Government, the fourth party, commonly establishes both the conditions under which fundamental infrastructure is provided and the regulatory requirements. It does this to fulfil obligations to citizens and varies with political perspective, economic ability and, of course, the constraints of physical geography. While no single approach to this provision can be universally applied, no single policy is applicable to all nations, the United Nations Sustainable Development Goals,[3] represents a minimum aspiration and requires provision of:

> Number 6: Clean Water and Sanitation;
>
> Number 7: Affordable and Clean Energy;
>
> Number 9: Industry, Innovation and Infrastructure;
>
> Number 11: Sustainable Cities and Communities.

These goals, adopted by the UN in 2015, seem proportionate and appropriate to an Intelligent Nation (which requires intelligent, resilient individuals) and are consistent with the UN Universal Declaration of Human Rights[4] which include

> Article 21: (2) Everyone has the right to equal access to public service in the country;
>
> Article 22: Everyone, as a member of society, has the right to social security and is entitled to realisation, through national effort and international co-operation and in accordance with the organisation and resources of each State, of the economic, social and cultural rights indispensable for their dignity and the free development of their personality.
>
> Article 25: (1) Everyone has the right to a standard of living adequate for the health and well-being of themselves and their family including food, clothing, housing, and medical care and necessary social services, and the right to security in the event of unemployment, sickness, disability, widowhood, old age or other lack of livelihood in circumstances beyond his control.

These things are seen as the responsibility of government to enable and provide, while nothing in either of these charters proposes either quantity or limit nor specifies the means by which they should be achieved. It is hard to see how, given the cost and impact on a country, that it could be created or sustained in the 21st century without government stimulus or intervention. Fundamental infrastructure is expensive with high initial and ongoing capital costs. The Australian Government 2019/20 Infrastructure Investment Programme[5] had a value of Aus$100 billion, while in the USA, a 2019 US$200 billion federal investment supporting a total US$1.5 trillion programme was shown by the independent Centre on Budget and Policy Priorities[6] to represent a reduction in spending and to be seen as a stimulus to State level investment. In the UK, the National Infrastructure Assessment (NIC, 2018) proposed a long-term governmental funding level equivalent to between 1.0 and 1.2 percent of GDP with a continuation of the shift towards a 'user pays' business model for certain aspects. The Infrastructure and Projects Authority, the body responsible for project delivery, reported (IPA, 2019), for its 2018/19-year projects a total, whole life, investment of £304 billion (excluding military projects).

Infrastructure investment has to be understood as value-enabling, creating the future for a country. Investment commonly extends over multiple generations with benefits that extend long into the future. The core of the London Underground is now well over 150 years old but, with appropriate maintenance, renewal and upgrade of equipment and vehicles, can be confidently expected to continue providing benefit for many years. The London sewer system devised by Bazalgette and opened in the 1860s has been in continuous operation ever since. The steam railway, pioneered on the Stockton to Darlington line in 1825, eventually extended across the entire UK with a full national network (Wolmar, 2007) in place by the end of the 1840s. In 2020, the UK Government committed to building 'HS2', a completely new railway providing additional connections between cities in the Midlands and North of England, terminating at Edinburgh, Glasgow and London. HS2 has benefit realisation extending 100 years beyond its start date with a capital cost estimated at around £100 billion at the time of writing and a 20-year build programme. Benefits cannot even begin to be realised for 10 years from commencement. Our cars, buses and lorries are driven on roads, particularly motorways and dual carriageways that have mainly been developed since the 1950s and will still be available to us for many generations. The costs and the timelines for benefit realisation are way beyond the capability of a risk priced, market-based investment approach to sustain, particularly when we consider that 'payback', which is dispersed across whole communities and multiple generations both locally and at a distance, can only be measured rather indirectly within the constraints of current evaluation models. We all believe infrastructure is a good thing; we know we rely upon it but proving the case is challenging.

Fundamental infrastructure is enabling; it exists to enable the well-being of the citizens of the nation, to facilitate their lives and the industries, agriculture, commerce that they pursue. It creates the value-enabling platform on which all of the value-generating activity of the nation can be built. The ownership and business models by which primary fundamental infrastructure might be originated, maintained and exploited are not, for an Intelligent Nation, a consideration in determining purpose but rather a secondary consideration. Exploring purpose is about considering the 'why' of the infrastructure, the business and ownership models are concerned with the 'how'. Fundamentally, a resilient infrastructure capable of meeting the requirements of the citizens, consistent with international (though not universally supported) agreements, should be thought of as a moral obligation in an Intelligent Nation.

Infrastructure ownership and business models

It can be argued that early infrastructures have their deepest origins in local market trading and travelling specialists followed, at least in Europe, by the marches of invading armies (we still follow Roman road routes across many parts of the continent). In the UK, it was only in the 17th and 18th centuries that the creation by Act of Parliament of Turnpike Trusts (Beckford P., unpublished) permitted managed investment in major travel routes; investment that was expected to generate increased income from rents and trading profits rather than directly from tolls which were intended to recover costs only. In many mature nations, the infrastructure has a history of government approved but privately initiated origins with subsequent nationalisation (sometimes associated with financial failure, sometimes not) and, most recently in many nations, a privatisation of some or all of the critical elements. In this history of ownership of infrastructure in mature economies, we can see that nations are commonly pulled between two unsatisfactory alternatives: private ownership and state ownership.

The primary responsibility of the Board for a company in private ownership is to act in the interests of the shareholders, usually taken to mean short-term maximisation of shareholder monetary value. Regulation ends up as a factor to be managed or 'gamed' by the Directors, regulations are observed but their weaknesses or inadequacies often exploited. Profits are extracted by dividend as investment returns to providers of equity and investment is minimised; no less than is necessary for the fulfilment of obligations, no more than can be justified by the increased returns to the shareholders; profit (value) is (notionally) maximised. Capital, for which there is global competition and where there is significant cost, is made available by way of equity or, quite commonly, loan by owners and their backers with a significant interest burden impacting on the long-term cost base of the provider. Where the capital provider is both provider of equity (shareholder) and loans, perhaps through a parent company arrangement, it can be argued that they are generating non-trading-related income by loaning rather than investing the bulk of the capital made available, the cost of finance becoming part of the financing cost of the business. This approach, which increases the gearing ratio of the company (the ratio of permanent capital to temporary capital), reduces the overall resilience of the company and can distort its apparent profitability. Lowering the reportable profit also has the effect of reducing tax obligations (especially if loans are made from alternative tax jurisdictions). This might be seen as a device for tax avoidance while also distorting the cost structure, especially if interest rates do not reflect open market conditions. It may be that the cost of capital provided by loan becomes a disincentive to investment, that is, inadequate permanent capital raises the cost of investment and thereby damages the case for it and/or increases the argument for either price rises or state subsidy. It might be considered that proposals to provide public funding to support infrastructure development in both the energy and transport sectors reflect this approach to funding by the owning groups. The fully private model requires economic regulation to protect the interests of the consumer and the taxpayer.

While a state-owned organisation can also have a profit focus, it may well do so acting as a sovereign investor. For example, the Singapore General Investment Corporation[7] handles investments designed to secure the future of that country with a value of around US$100 billion spread across 40 countries and generating long-term sustainable returns. Such funds can be regarded for all practical purposes as any other investor and exist in a variety of countries. It is notable that both France and Germany have declared intent to increase their investments in strategic industries as part of the recovery plan from the Covid-19 pandemic.

Nationalisation[8] by contrast occurs when a State directly takes over the ownership, with or without compensation, of an organisation. This is sometimes rooted in an act of purely political belief in state ownership for public benefit and sometimes it is a mechanism for preserving or protecting an industry, a set of assets or for preserving employment. The common, though not universal, consequences of full nationalisation are low capital investment, relative inefficiency, production focus rather than consumption focus, challenges in incentivising performance. A swathe of nationalisations has happened over many years from Royal Dutch and Standard Oil in 1938 to General Motors in the USA and Royal Bank of Scotland following the financial crash in 2008. The drivers and motivations have varied as have the results. In the UK a range of nationalisations undertaken shortly after the end of World War II were largely reversed in the 1980s and 1990s with the whole or partial privatisation of utilities (water, gas, electricity, telecommunications, airlines), while other nationalised industries declined further (ship-building, coal mining, steel-making), having been overtaken in some respects by lower cost providers from other countries. Some of those lower costs reflected cheaper labour and energy, some arose from innovations and mechanisation not adopted in the UK, leaving the industries lagging. Some part of the reason for that may well have been a lack of capital available for investment as emphasis shifted to the social infrastructure of education, health and social care. This is a common though not a necessary outcome of nationalisation.

Much depends on the rationale of a government in nationalising the industry, its capability in management (as opposed to administration) and its appetite for risk. The obligation of the Board is to meet whatever objectives and challenges are set for it by government and to work within whatever budget is allocated. The Government (whether National or Local) is likely to constrain the organisation to work within financial time frames influenced heavily by electoral and fiscal cycles and in which, given always competing priorities, capital investment is likely to be lacking. The absence of market pressures around performance can lead to such organisations becoming inefficient or sustaining inefficient working and production practices, because the cost of change is outside the scope of the available budget. It should be noted here that such constraints on capital are not unique to nationalised industry. They have been observed in private, public and third-sector organisations in industries ranging from food production to paper making, to the provision of social care. For a nationalised organisation though, public benefit is (notionally) maximised. Inefficient, subsidised industries are unlikely to attract or even be open to investment from the sort of sovereign investment funds mentioned above.

Experience of both types of ownership bears out the remarks which apply as much to energy and water (clean and waste) as they do to transport (rail and bus in particular) and its infrastructure (airports, etc). Neither private nor public ownership appears to offer a 'best fit' solution. The ideal would perhaps be to resolve the tensions between 'maximising profit' and 'maximising public benefit' not by posing them as alternatives but as complementary. The traditional ownership models do not allow for this, but can perhaps do so if we deal with the interests of investors as actors in the situation. We need to consider the alignment of investor interest with those of consumers, government, regulators. In an Intelligent Nation, of sufficient political, social and economic maturity, access to and availability of clean water, disposal of waste and availability of energy can reasonably be considered not just markers of civilisation but fundamental human rights (consistent with the UN charter already cited). We have to give thought in such circumstances to the potential for alternative models based on aligned interests and non-governmental community ownership, a form of social enterprise such as has been growing in occurrence and importance particularly in post-industrial economies.

One such organisation is New Holstein Utilities in Wisconsin, USA, one of around 2200 such public utility companies in the USA. Owned by its community it provides power, water and wastewater services. Its charges are based on a cost-recovery model and its 'Utility Commission' (the equivalent of the Board) is comprised of four citizens plus a Council nominee. It is run by a professional executive. In a survey[9] the approach was lionised by the public:

> A majority of U.S. consumers believe that public power is more concerned about the environment, offers lower rates, allows more control over utility operations and has better service than private power companies. The public believes local ownership of electric utilities plays a strong role in the electric industry.

There are a number of challenges that arise when we consider scaling up the idea of community ownership from small-town USA (New Holstein has a population of around 2600) to a national scale proposition, not least the potential increase in the number of interdependencies that might be created. It is clear that there is also a risk of creating the sort of monolithic organisations commonly associated with nationalisation and failing to realise the benefits of the change. Similarly, there would be a substantial task in raising and sustaining the capital required not just for ownership but, more significantly, for the level of sustained investment necessary to maintain performance. Executives would continue to need to be of the highest professional calibre and the traditional incentive of stock options would not be available. Such an organisation, owned by its customers and operated on their behalf but in their interest, would need to be capable of generating a surplus for reinvestment in itself and to balance the need for a lean, cost and performance-oriented approach with one which ensured adequate resilience. Interestingly, the US 'Institute for Local Self-Reliance' (Farrell, 2016) report 'Beyond Sharing' states that 'Danish wind projects are typically owned by several to several hundred landowners and farmers in "wind partnerships". The result is that 20% of Denmark's power comes from wind, and 85% of that is owned by the residents of Danish communities'. Clearly community ownership can work.

Towards a future ownership model

We need to set aside existing arrangements from our thinking and consider from an Intelligent Nation perspective not what we have but what we want. Whatever the starting point, the consideration of policy is surely to think about what best suits the requirements. When we think globally about fundamental infrastructure and take account of natural justice and equity that would require fair access for all together with the goals for both sustainable living and human rights, then it seems that many of our current arrangements cannot suffice. It may be that the pursuit of sustainable infrastructure acquires new emphasis in a post Covid-19 world especially for less advantaged countries[10]. In many developing nations, there are limited water supplies and little if any sewerage or electrical supply. In industrialised and post-industrial nations, notwithstanding awesome wealth in many respects, there are still significant parts of the population living in energy and water poverty (despite the legal inhibition across Europe that, in principle, prevents domestic water supply being terminated). In addition to this for some nations, there is an issue of digital exclusion, some citizens having insufficient money to be full participants in the emerging digital economies whether that be for access to goods, public services or entertainment. A system must be developed in which, at the least, the fundamental services are available to all across the economic spectrum.

To avoid the risks of monolithic bureaucracy, it seems that commissioning provision of these elements should be at a relatively local, perhaps community level. In the UK, that might be undertaken at or around local authority level, serving coherent communities. To develop an appropriate size and a resilient architecture such authorities might, in a limited way, band together. The limited way must ensure that there is a clear sense of local ownership and influence such that local people feel a sense of local control and can demonstrably exercise it, although the local authority must not be the dominant or controlling body. The strong interdependencies between fundamental infrastructure elements must be reflected and integrated services (say energy, water, sewerage, telecommunications) considered where required or desired. This undertaking would be community owned, perhaps fashioned along the lines of the New Holstein or Danish examples. Critically, these should be in the form of Community Interest Companies or Trusts managed on a not-for-profit basis. This of course could not meet all the requirements of managing, for example, a national grid for electricity distribution, but systems of such scale could be commissioned by or through the local organisations. Where large-scale production is required, for example, very large power-generation stations, these could continue to be commissioned through and with the financial support of national government but governed through a board wholly independent of government to have decision cycles independent of electoral concerns, that is, provision of fundamental infrastructure should not be a function of politics but of citizen or national demand. Students of infrastructure decisions in the UK will be only too aware of how electoral needs interfere with decision-making and clearly a mechanism (perhaps like jury service) will need to be created so that decision power for such utilities does not simply rest in the same hands as local civil administration by limiting individuals to holding only one elected office at any time.

National government would have three further roles to play in this arena. First is the duty of government to handle the necessary redistribution of wealth across a nation that ensures that local areas are not denuded of essential facilities and capabilities regardless of the source of deprivation. No economy can be balanced without such intervention while levelling up will always be one of the duties of central government. Second is to provide the nation with resilience in its provision. The market may provide, but even with community-owned organisations will only ever provide just enough and just in time; it will do what is economically viable. The third duty of the government is to provide capacity for 'just in case' and this might mean holding a strategic 'resilience share'[11] in all utility organisations, partly to support resilience, partly to preserve ownership in a form that supports the national interest.

In the early months of 2020 amid the throes of the Coronavirus Covid-19 pandemic, numerous governments fell short in that regard. System resilience must act not just to ensure that the needs of the whole nation can be met, even under challenging circumstances, but to give national government a voice, though not a controlling one, in the direction of the organisation with the opportunity to guide certain decisions in the national interest. An example might be to support the development of new, low-carbon power-generation capabilities that might be considered too risky or unproven for a commercial operator to develop as an investment proposition, but could be justified with that risk mitigated. The government as investor could secure the national interest, perhaps create a member board on the 'jury' principle and independent professional advisers could be appointed to the member board and disbarred from any other involvement in the enterprise.

Capital requirements for large-scale power-generation, distribution systems or transport projects are substantial and generate significant financial risk or extended time between investment and return. Governments are the only true providers of such capital whether through direct investment, loans, subsidies, underwriting of costs or guaranteed revenue. However much it may be proclaimed that the infrastructure is private, the risk is public. Mazzucato (2018) points to this extensively in considering the research and development domains. At least one part of the solution rests in the long-term relative stability of such organisations and consequently the potential for raising capital via bonds and debentures with fixed rather than market rate interest costs. Like government stocks these could be tradable allowing investors to participate in and support appropriate long-term investment while as Trusts or Community Interest Companies, they would not have shares for trading. Since the real value of the business is in its assets and its enabling role for society, this would seem a more appropriate way of sustaining capital and at a fixed cost, appealing to pension schemes and investors seeking long-term stability rather than speculation. Capital growth would be feasible through discounting of the bonds or debentures as with government stocks. Overall, such a model would be similar to the Housing Associations established in the UK which own and manage substantial stock of social housing, maintaining asset value with planned investment programmes over a 30-year view while not being available for exploitation. As with Housing Associations, it would be critical to employ a professional management team and to incentivise and reward them appropriately. These are serious businesses and must be directed and managed accordingly to deliver the outcomes desired by their community owners. The trick would be to optimise performance for all while managing the costs of the business, so as to sustain affordability and manage non-payment risk across the whole portfolio of users, both personal and commercial. Pricing would be set on a 'cost-recovery' basis with any surpluses reinvested in social provision (potentially eliminating water and energy poverty) or further investment in improving the effectiveness of the provision (more output, lower cost, etc.).

Summary

With the 'stock' in fundamental infrastructure organisations owned by the communities, a member council selected and overseeing the work of a professional management, capital raised via bonds and debentures and rewarded by interest payments, it would be feasible to deliver a local, resilient and integrated fundamental infrastructure. Such an approach could extend across the whole sector of energy, water, waste, transport and ICT. All would be managed in the interest of the Intelligent Nation and be integrated to manage interdependency and resilient to both internal and external perturbations.

Key points

- There are five fundamental infrastructure sub-systems: water, waste, energy, ICT, transport;
- Largely owned and operated separately, they are highly inter-connected and interdependent and in an Intelligent Nation must be managed as a whole system;

- Functional management of infrastructure sub-systems renders them liable to single point of failure and cascade failure risk;
- Fundamental infrastructure assets and networks are critical to national resilience; they are not just technical artefacts but enablers of social infrastructure and society;
- The criticality of any asset is dynamic, varying with the topology of its multiple networks and the criticality of all the other networks and assets and the environmental conditions:
- Infrastructure investment has a multi-generational payback and is unsuited to conventional business models and financial evaluation techniques;
- Alternative business models, including community ownership-based approaches, may offer a more sustainable approach to building and maintaining infrastructure.

References

Beer, S., (1985) *Diagnosing the System for Organisations*, Wiley, Chichester

Council on Science and Technology, (2009) *An Infrastructure for the 21st Century*, HMSO, London, UK

Dolan, T., (2017) *Digitally connected infrastructure system resilience: literature review (UCL)*, National Infrastructure Commission, Ove Arup & Partners Ltd, London. https://www.nic.org.uk/wp-content/uploads/CCCC17A21-Project-Literature-Review.pdf

Farrell, J., (2016) *Beyond Sharing*, Institute for Local Self-Reliance, Washington, USA

Hasan, S. and Foliente, G., (2015) Modeling infrastructure system interdependencies and socioeconomic impacts of failure in extreme events: emerging R&D challenges, *Natural Hazards*, 78(3), pp. 2143–2168. doi: 10.1007/s11069-015-1814-7.

Infrastructure and Projects Authority, (2019) *Annual Report on Major Projects 2018–19*, Crown Copyright

Mazzucato, M., (2018) *The Value of Everything*, Penguin, London Books, New York

National Infrastructure Commission, (2018) *National Infrastructure Assessment*, National Infrastructure Commission, London

Perrow, C., (1999) *Normal accidents: living with high risk technologies*, Princeton University Press, New Jersey, USA

President's Commission, (1997) *Critical foundations: protecting America's infrastructure*, Federation of American Scientists, Washington, USA

Rinaldi, S.M., et al. (2001) Identifying, Understanding and Analysing Critical infrastructure interdependencies, *IEEE Control Systems Magazine*, 0272-1708/01, USA

Stirling, A., (2010) Keep it complex. *Nature*, 468, pp. 1029–1031

Wolmar, C., (2007) *Fire & Steam: How the Railways Transformed Britain*, Atlantic Books, London

Notes

1. https://beckfordconsulting.com/wp-content/uploads/2019/11/Modernising-National-Infrastructure-Draft-2009.pdf 06/04/2020
2. https://beckfordconsulting.com/wp-content/uploads/2018/12/Asset-Criticality-Modelling.pdf 12/04/2020
3. https://www.undp.org/content/undp/en/home/sustainable-development-goals.html 20/04/2020

4. https://www.ohchr.org/EN/UDHR/Documents/UDHR_Translations/eng.pdf 20/04/2020

5. https://investment.infrastructure.gov.au/ 21/04/2020

6. https://www.cbpp.org/research/state-budget-and-tax/its-time-for-states-to-invest-in-infrastructure 21/04/2020

7. https://www.gic.com.sg/about-gic/ 23/04/2020

8. https://www.investopedia.com/terms/n/nationalization.asp 23/4/2020

9. https://www.nhutilities.org/local-ownership 23/04/2020

10. https://blogs.iadb.org/sostemibilidad/en/four-reasons-why-civil-society-should-support-sustainable-infrastructire-post-covid-19/ 20/04/2020

11. https://beckfordconsulting.com/wp-content/uploads/2019/11/Infrastructure-Resilience-Matters.pdf 20/06/2020

6

UNDERSTANDING PERFORMANCE, SERVING CITIZENS RIGHT

Introduction

Contemporary means and methods of reporting on national performance are rather traditional and require a radical shift in approach. The traditional, purely economic view is clearly not adequate for an Intelligent Nation as a complex adaptive system. If the Intelligent Nation is to survive and thrive, it must have self-determining and appropriately supported citizens and achieve democratically informed harmony between citizens and state over social, economic and environmental priorities. That harmony must be sustained in diverse international relationships. It must achieve a sustainable balance of society, economy and environment and, with probity and integrity, attain a prudent level of state (national, regional and local) spending and investment as a proportion of the total economy.

Performance beyond GDP

Gross Domestic Product (GDP) is the measure in traditional economics of the final monetary value of goods and services produced in a nation in a given time period. It is the measure by which nations report whether their wealth has increased or decreased by comparison with the previous period and indicates relative economic position in an index of nations. One of its problems is that we are never really comparing like with like. Mazzucato (2018) points out that the basis of calculation evolves over time, the range of things included in the calculation changes and, in models that economists have created, the 'production boundary', the imaginary line between the sub-system of 'productive activities' and the sub-system of 'unproductive activities', moves so that different versions accommodate different economic theories. Essentially, 'productive' activities are considered as things that generate wealth, while 'unproductive' activities are those which primarily deal with redistributions of wealth or extract 'rents' (charges and interest for the use of assets such as property and money) also called unearned income by some. What is in debate in economics is which activities fall into which category, what should be asked is whether the categorisation is useful. The ideas of value-enabling and value-generating activities have been discussed throughout this text, recognising the mutual interdependence and, ultimately, the inseparability of the two things from a systemic perspective, perhaps that is more useful? This book will not try to settle the economists' disagreements that would need several other books. It will instead take the position that if economists can't agree what GDP is then why, and how, do they think they can measure it and what does it mean when they do.

What Mazzucato establishes quite clearly is that although some activities appear to take place on the productive side of the economists' boundary, they are often funded, stimulated, supported, sponsored or subsidised by organisations, commonly governments but sometimes foundations and charities, on the unproductive side, that is, value-enabling activity is supporting and stimulating value-generating activity, just as the Intelligent Organisation would expect. Mazzucato points to numerous examples over many years from information technology, space exploration, defence, telecommunications and pharmaceutical industries as supporting her perspective. There are numerous other examples, particularly in research and development across many fields, where state or third sector actors, such as universities, have taken 'mission-oriented' research funded by the state and exploited it for productive (commercial) gain, the shareholders benefitting from the activity and, eventually, the state through taxation. Taxation provides the conventional mechanism by which public services are funded and economic redistribution is achieved. Initially taxes (tithes usually paid in kind in mediaeval systems) were levied by landowners, monarchs and emperors, later by governments on income, subsequently on capital growth and wealth transfer, more recently on expenditure at both local and national levels. Governments and local authorities use the tax revenue in its various forms to fund services to and for the public which are free at the point of delivery, although they may be delivered via public, private, charitable or social organisations. Over the last 100 or so years, they have used some proportion of it to redistribute wealth and support the less fortunate in our societies, while much tax revenue has supported the research and development undertaken by university and other researchers as highlighted in Mazzucato's research. There is a vast body of legislation globally that seeks to capture these tax revenues and an equally vast body of case law and knowledgeable experts, whose task is to defeat or avoid the legislation. Clearly something is not working when private beneficiaries do not support the totality of the private and public system from which they benefit, including contributing to the cost of the innovations which have enabled their success.

Mazzucato establishes systemic interdependence between the wealth-generation activity of the productive organisations and the redistribution and investment activity of the unproductive, in particular governments. The seemingly false demarcation between the two becomes critical when viewed through the lens of the Intelligent Organisation, not because it defines one part as being useful and the other not, but because it helps us to understand the dynamic complexity of the contemporary economic and social systems and the complementarity of the parts. It is important to remember that systemic emergence depends not simply on the performance of those parts, but on the interactions between them. Thinking about the Intelligent Nation as a complex adaptive system, it is simply not meaningful in a contemporary economy to attribute 'productiveness' to only one set of activities. Rather, we must comprehend that the productiveness of an economy is an emergent property of the interactions and interdependence of all of the actors, whether state, private or third sector in that economy, and in other dependent relationships internationally. Accumulated wealth, the sustained excess of income over expenditure over time, results from the interactions of those actors and somehow its distribution needs to more adequately reflect that.

Systemic reporting: Managing the whole

Raworth (2018) argues from a systemic perspective that GDP is inadequate and, in its stead, proposes the notion of 'doughnut economics'. In the centre of the inner ring of her doughnut, the Social Foundation, is what Raworth calls 'Critical Human Deprivation' – a level to which we should not allow any individual to sink. Outside the outer ring, the Ecological Ceiling, she describes 'Critical Planetary Degradation' in which as a result of human activity, the planet experiences traumatic climate change and loss of biodiversity. Between these two extremes is the 'Safe and Just Space for Humanity', a morally informed idealised state of being. Supporting this proposition, Raworth argues for a set of ways of achieving this, many of them themes already encountered in this book. They include moving the perceived goal from a pure focus on GDP to a more sustainable position balanced between the foundation and the ceiling; understanding the big picture of the world as a system with all of its dynamic complexity and interactions and acting on a more human, socially engaged agenda. Suggesting that we are 'addicted' to growth, Raworth proposes redesigning our organisations so that the profits of success are distributed by design and that sustainability and regeneration should be embedded in the business processes. The OECD (1975) sets out the 'polluter pays principle' that this reflects, although it might now be considered more appropriate for the polluter to prevent, restore or rectify damage than to compensate for it. The critical idea in all of this is the shift from a single target for performance to a more complex, more nuanced way of thinking. The challenge to the pursuit of growth is of real importance here and was discussed by Meadows et al. (1972) in 'Limits to Growth' primarily in relation to the environmental damage being done to the planet by all forms of human activity.

Beckford (2020) suggests that there are two dimensions of growth: the physiological and the psychological. Focusing on the first of these, while acknowledging the sharp intake of breath it will cause in certain circles, physiological growth (getting bigger) is not necessarily a long-term survival strategy. For human beings there is most likely and unique to each of us, a 'right size' or 'best size', one at which we balance height, weight and width, sustaining that position with a balance of energy input to energy expended. The excess in the human case turns to fat; when we become fat, we become slower, less agile, less able to adapt, more susceptible to diseases, more likely to die early. Organisations are similar; when they reach maturity and particularly in an oligopoly or monopoly market position, they wax fat on the profits and become cautious in defending their position; bureaucracy (the system of 'offices' that consistently delivers the things we already know how to do) grows. Failure to invest in alternatives is good news for emerging competitors in that it renders the incumbent vulnerable. A healthy position for an organisation might be to be just successful enough. Adaptation and energy maintained, it would earn more than it needs to spend, provide a reasonable return on invested capital and, most critically, invest sufficient of its surplus in adapting or re-inventing itself that it ensures its own survival. It never becomes complacent. Psychological maturity appears in that ability to recognise both that the current size, shape and position is sustainable and that the key to survival is continuing adaptation, persistent dynamic rebalancing. Surplus assets, not required to sustain the position, can be returned to investors, invested in other propositions, shared with those who make the surplus possible, distributed. In essence, the Intelligent Organisation grows in both dimensions. It grows its savings (the surplus of income over expenditure) by adapting its processes to be more efficient in pursuit of current goals. Keeping the same nominal size but using less resources is a different growth, one which resides in the other dimension, that of psychological growth. They don't just get bigger, they get smarter, cleverer, more efficient and more effective. Beckford (2020) cites the example of the social enterprise Fusion21 which over 5 years, in adopting the ideas of Intelligent Organisation maintained its workforce at the same level but doubled its turnover, trebled its financial bottom line, reduced its environmental impact and, through its owning foundation, invested the surplus in a range of projects for social value, delivering improvement for the people and communities it serves. It is suggested that an Intelligent Nation could work the same way, getting bigger and smarter in parallel. This cannot be achieved when GDP is the only measure of success.

These arguments take us closer to the idea of the triple bottom line, the idea that an organisation can simultaneously deliver financial, social and environmental benefits. Elkington (Henriques and Richardson, 2004) describes how the idea of a triple bottom line emerged in about 1994 from a survey concerned with corporate social responsibility and sustainable development and focused on 'seven sustainability revolutions'. Elkington describes these seven as a shift in:

- markets from compliance to competition;
- values from hard to soft;
- transparency from closed to open;
- technology life-cycles from products to features;
- partnerships from subversion to symbiosis;
- timing from short term to long term;
- governance from exclusive to inclusive.

It is probably fair to say that at the time of writing, some of these shifts have not been fully realised, in some cases not started. It is especially true that shifts in technology and buyer behaviour, particularly from outright purchase to renting, have enabled the emergence of oligopolistic, near monopoly, positions in some markets which have inhibited competition rather than encouraged it. Meanwhile, notwithstanding the shock of the 2008 financial crisis, there has not yet been a profound shift to thinking about organisational or national performance in terms of the triple bottom line, nor does it appear likely such a shift will occur soon, although governmental responses to the Coronavirus pandemic of 2020 may change that. While the proposed change in thinking, similar to Raworth, has merit, reflecting aspects of Taguchi's (1987) quadratic loss function, 'the loss imparted to society from the time a product is shipped', it does not integrate the three aspects, considering them more as alternatives to offset than as an integrated system in which change in each has implications for the others.

The measurement or regulation of any system will focus attention on it and stimulate a change in behaviour; the action of measurement always distorts the system. Braithwaite (2008) suggests that since the 1970s, we in the UK have become engaged in a form of 'regulatory capitalism', a form of governmental interventionist behaviour which neither adds nor detracts value from the economy but rather seeks to influence it in the direction preferred by the government of the day. There are numerous challenges with such an approach, not least that by the time government has collected data, filtered and interpreted it and considered it through the lens of its own particular political narrative, its intervention is too late and has changed the system. The consequence of late intervention is often to amplify difference that should be damped and damp difference that should be amplified. Rather than resolve an undesired oscillation both booms and busts get amplified or exaggerated by government intervention. Meanwhile, according to Lev-Faur et al. cited by Braithwaite (2008), the 'scope, arenas, instruments and depths' of regulation increase.

Governance in a complex adaptive system

Governance is integral to nurturing the complex adaptive system that is an Intelligent Nation. The Intelligent Nation exhibits dynamic and probabilistic behaviour and its governance needs to embrace the words of Maton[1] that 'in a democratic society people have a right to regulate the problems capitalism creates, and shape the problems that it solves. Markets don't operate in a social or environmental vacuum'. This requires that one of the things we evaluate and govern is the stewardship of the democracy itself and that is carried out through the electoral processes.

Turning to the economy, Maton cites Beinhocker's (2007) view that 'If we invented economics today from scratch, it would look nothing like what you see in textbooks', while Lord Toby Harris[2] discussing post-Covid19 London argues for 'E[3]' (Economy, Equity, Environment) and asserts that no single interest can prosper at the expense of others. There are a number of elements not accounted for in the ideas for managing performance we have so far considered. First, they do not explicitly embrace the ideas of localisation, regionalisation and devolution or decentralisation, they are primarily national in conception. We should measure our autonomy and act to sustain it. Second, while Raworth talks about 'society', Mazzucato discusses sources of wealth and Elkington talks of societal benefits, none talks enough of the necessary role of the citizen in determining the meaning of value nor of the mechanisms of engagement essential to enabling everyone to contribute to relevant decisions. None consider the obligations of a government to govern, the powers that electors lend them to do so, the hierarchy of governance that necessarily emerges and the consequent need for ongoing reaffirmation of democratic legitimacy. Obligations and powers are reserved to a government through its constitutional structure, whether formal as in the case of most modern nations, or evolutionary and fluid as in the UK; the tension between governmental and electoral power needs to be managed. What is needed is a more comprehensive approach to understanding national performance. That approach needs to synthesise the multiple dimensions of performance, be aggregated from the individual view through the emergent hierarchy of local and regional perspectives to national government so as to allow for both distributed and centralised decisions to be competently taken. It must integrate the different dimensions of performance to constitute a purposeful whole reflecting the nation back to itself. The result will have the support of the citizens for whose benefit, guidance and information it is produced.

Any living or dynamical system (and an Intelligent Nation must be thought of as both) is sustainable within a particular set of parameters in concert with its environment; its host. That environment is also changing such that sustainability becomes joint and several, interdependent and co-evolutionary. Change in either the system itself or its environment that takes either outside its parameters of sustainability will initially compromise performance and ultimately kill the system, the environment or both. Lovelock (1995) referred to this at planetary level in his 'Gaia Hypothesis' suggesting that while planet earth will survive, conditions on it may not always support human life. Reflecting on the growth, decline and fall of empires through history and the equivalent by companies in industries which emerge, grow, dominate then ultimately fail, it is not a stretch to consider how such thinking might apply to contemporary nations and that a better way is needed. A richer, integrated, holistic mechanism is required for understanding the multidimensional well-being of individuals, locations, regions and nations in order that more informed decisions can be made.

Risk arises in attempts at measurement, first in understanding what is to be measured and why. Second, risk arises in the compilation, presentation and interpretation of the measurements. The outbreak of the Coronavirus Covid-19 and the subsequent reporting highlighted weaknesses in the ability of several countries to record accurately, interpret consistently and report faithfully those things chosen for measurement. It may be that the evaluation needs to be expressed in non-quantitative terms, that there is a need to become accustomed to only understanding improvement or deterioration in a situation rather than seeking the illusory certainty of a particular metric. Waddington (1977) explains this through the idea of searching an epigenetic landscape in which every step is taken not towards an absolute but towards 'better', defined as observably closer to a chosen destination or fulfilment of a purpose.

The following study was written at the height of the Covid-19 Pandemic in early 2020 when the cause and pathway of the virus were poorly understood, when governments were of necessity making policy up on the fly and when much of the population in many countries had been confined to their homes to reduce propagation risk. Meanwhile the timing of the onset of the pandemic and governmental response in each country meant that some governments appeared to be more, or less, successful than others in their actions while much information available to the public was speculative rather than factual.

Covid-19: The necessity of evolving wisdom: Dr. John Beckford[3]

I have previously confessed to spending a little too much time acquiring information from diverse sources. However, after one exposition on a well-known mainstream news channel I realised that I actually knew less after the programme than I did at the start.

Stories about Covid-19 from all over the world have a multiplicity of platforms, channels, networks and even newspapers on which to propagate – and there is neither transmission inhibitor nor vaccine! Once we are on line we are exposed.

One of the main themes, at least here in the UK, is stories which purport to compare the inadequate performance of the government of Country A (the host country) with the amazing performance of the government of Country B (any other country – or even several of them). In such a case, a number reported (I hesitate to call them metrics) is worse in Country A than it is in Country B.

We have all become familiar with the international league tables of deaths and recovery rates, the test rates for various categories of citizens, virus reproduction rates and the assorted speculations over antigen tests, antibody tests, post-infection immunity, viral load and the efficacy, or not, of experimental treatments and prophylactics including face masks, social distancing, self-isolation and the militaristically toned 'lockdown'.

But:

We are seeking certainty where none exists, nor can it (yet) exist.

Why:

Not enough is yet known, by anyone, about the virus itself to provide certainty of almost anything

And:

We are making comparisons where none is meaningful, nor can they (yet) be meaningful!

Because:

Comparisons made are often not appropriately underpinned by a comprehension and appreciation of differences:

Countries vary in their approach to recording primary cause of death:
> The basis of recording and reporting of illness and death varies from country to country; are people dying purely OF Covid-19 or of some pre-existing morbidity but while infected WITH Covid-19;

The timing of recording and reporting varies from country to country;

The impact of infected patients' pre-existing conditions on the course of the virus is not fully understood;

Testing regimes vary substantially;

The effectiveness of therapeutic techniques is not fully understood:
> PPE, ventilators, CPAP devices, intensity of care, existing drugs (or their absence), the physical conditions of the hospital itself

The skills, experience, insight of clinicians is variable;

Differences in a wide variety of life circumstances are not factored in to gross comparisons:
> Population Density, Domestic Circumstances, Living Conditions, Working Conditions, Population Age Profile, Diet and Nutrition, Alcohol and Tobacco Consumption, Co-morbidities, Occupations.

I could go on.

The welter of stories is amplified to a tsunami by the apparent desperate need among news providers to 'keep the public informed' during the current pandemic. The curious might wonder about the real purposes of the various stories, in the meanwhile we should work on the assumptions:

> Scientists, everywhere, are doing their very best to provide their governments with the best information and advice they can give;
> In a rapidly evolving situation it is inevitable, indeed it is to be expected, that some of that advice will change over time;
> Different scientists in different countries drawing on different data will arrive at different advice and recommendations;
> It is inevitable; indeed, it is to be expected, that governments will be differently advised;

Governments, everywhere, are doing their very best to provide their countries with the best decisions, guidance, information, social and economic outcomes that can be achieved in the light of the evidence they have received;

Given different advice it should be no surprise that governments make different judgements and do different things;

In a rapidly evolving situation it is inevitable, indeed it is to be expected, that some of the decisions, guidance, information, social and economic outcomes will change over time.

A useful working assumption is that every scientist and politician is authentically and persistently making the best recommendations and decisions they can in the light of the information available at the time. If when the information changes, they make a different decision, that does not mark a failure of the previous position but their evolving knowledge which we experience as wisdom.

However inept, however right or wrong in their decision-making our politicians and scientists appear in retrospect, let us not underestimate the challenge of decision-making under conditions of uncertainty.

Measurement and judgement

All measurement needs a what, a how and a why, all relative to the definition of success and viability. Any measure which does not contribute to understanding and managing that sustainability is moot at best. Each unit of measurement needs a clear operational definition, a standard or norm that gives it consistency of meaning along with recognition that in deciding on the metrics the world that can be seen is being defined and delineated. It sometimes matters less how something is defined as long as it is done consistently and there is agreement about its meaning even when measurement is problematic. Huff (1991) suggests that numbers, in particular, the presentation of statistics, are used to colour our interpretation of matters, while Muller (2018) talks about 'The Tyranny of Metrics' suggesting, among many other things that 'what gets measured gets gamed'. Muller points out that when things are chosen for measurement then those responsible for the activities that generate the result may well adapt their behaviour to ensure the number is that which is expected. In other words, measuring and counting distorts the result. When considering the performance of a dynamical system, thinking is needed about more than one aspect of performance. What is needed is not just the result of a measurement taken at any given point in time but also the rate and direction of change in that measurement AND the change in the environment, such triangulation helping with comprehension of the meaning and validity of the result. Confidence is needed that the accuracy of measurement means that any decision made using the information provided is appropriate. That is no mean feat and it cannot be done in a centralised, uni-dimensional model.

Muller makes a second point, one which in many respects has a more profound consequence than the first. Over many years the ability to obtain measurements has become seductive, even obsessional, especially in the days of the 'Internet of Things'. The emergence of 'big data' in particular has accelerated the tendency for often spurious accuracy arising from our counting of things to replace human judgement in decision-making. In effect in many instances, the data have been inappropriately allowed to drive the decision. Expert judgement needs to be restored to decision-making, data must be used to generate a platform for decision that informs but does not replace judgement, so that measurement can inform the thinking not BE the thinking. Uncertainty is inherent in dynamic and complex situations, so the exercise of judgement is both essential and heuristic. There will always be a gap between those things chosen for measurement, the ways chosen to measure them (which between them constitute a model of the situation) and the situation as it is experienced and understood by others. Measurements are always less rich than the situation observed; any interpretation is always an abstraction from the total information content of any particular model filtered by knowledge, skill, experience, insight with choices informed by assumptions, biases and prejudices. Accepting that the model cannot represent the totality of the situation demands acceptance of the exercise of judgement which, in turn, demands investment in the ability of individuals to develop judgement, to learn from experience. In hindsight, some judgements may be wrong, that is in their nature but human beings are extremely good at learning to reduce error over multiple iterations. In making decisions, information received from appropriate quantitative measurement must be balanced with judgement based on the explicable, defensible and qualitative, with action on the result and learning from mistakes.

Ideally, measurement should occur as a by-product or consequence of processes rather than as a separate activity, measuring in particular (and in however many dimensions are necessary for accuracy) whether or not the intended outcome was achieved. Note here the emphasis is on outcome not output; it is not what was done that really matters, it is what was achieved and the context of that achievement. It is achievement of outcome that is the mark of effectiveness; this gives meaning to the output which is the measure of efficiency.

The homeostat: A governance device

The homeostat (Figure 6.1) begins to outline the performance mechanisms of the Intelligent Nation approach. To achieve a given societal outcome, a process or operation (with standards and a specification) is carried out using a variety of inputs (e.g. labour, materials, data, energy) and generates outputs (e.g. product or service, waste,

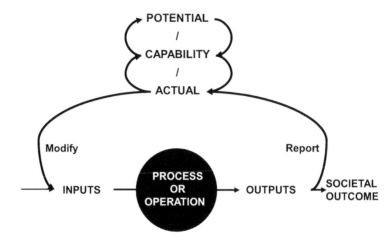

FIGURE 6.1 The homeostat

data, etc) intended to fulfil the expectation. The homeostat captures data about the process (ACTUAL) which is then compared with the standards and specification (CAPABILITY), a statement of the best that can be done with the existing process design, systems, resources and other inputs.

If the ACTUAL performance does not equal the CAPABILITY then modification is made to the next cycle of inputs in order to close the gap. The measurement and corrective action are thereby embedded in the operation; the process self-manages and improves with each cycle. Analogous to the regulator on a steam engine, in going out of control, the system brings itself back into control.

At the higher level, the current CAPABILITY is compared with the POTENTIAL (a future-oriented statement of what could be done if the process design, system, resources or other constraints were changed), a statement of aspiration or intent. If CAPABILITY does not equal POTENTIAL, then modification is made to it in order to close the gap. Again, the measurement is built into the system, double loops of learning through reporting and corrective action are embedded; the system becomes both self-regulating and inherently adaptive. It is cybernetic by design; in the process of failing it will correct itself. The higher order measure describes the latent capability of the process, the lower order measure its current productivity or efficiency.

Using this process homeostat as the basis of performance understanding, we can use the information feedback (corrective) and feedforward (anticipatory) to regulate the organisation and, because measurement is embedded in the specification of the system itself, with agreed specifications, we minimise the risk of Mullers 'tyranny' and 'gaming'. The system itself, the process with its embedded performance management, is designed to be goal-seeking at two levels of consideration: the present and the future. The next case shows how these ideas work at a practical level.

Intelligent emergency care: Dr. Charles House

Driving quality and performance improvement through a reflective cycle is to measure actual performance against a capability, understand the gap and then adjust the inputs (be they skills, materials, tasks or processes) at the next iteration or cycle, in order to close the gap between the two.

At the time of writing for emergency admissions to UCLH we have a clear performance standard to meet, namely 95% of patients either admitted or discharged from the Emergency Department (ED) within 4 hours. On a daily basis, we understand only too well what the gap is, we know by how far we have come up short of hitting the 95% mark.

For some components of the overall process NHS centrally mandated standards exist, against which we measure performance, for example Time to Initial Assessment and Time to Treatment. Processes, pathways and staffing levels are tweaked and flexed in response to underperformance in the relevant areas in the continuing attempt to close the gap between actual and desired performance.

For other aspects of care and interventions along the patient pathway, we set our own internal standards and expectations. Some of these, such as the turnaround time for blood test results to become available, can be agreed between a relatively small number of stakeholders and be measured with relative ease. Others involve more teams and are subject to less sophisticated data capture, for instance the time taken from referral for a patient to be seen by a specialist team.

So, while some steps of a care pathway can be and indeed are measured and monitored, it is nevertheless hard to provide a systematic higher order action designed to improve the overall process so that the performance gap is always being reduced. Daily variance in performance suggests a process that is not 'in control', with insufficient damping of variation between best and worst performance.

Our challenge is to understand how best to address this, to reduce variation and improve overall performance? One approach is to be clear about what things are within our control and to ask teams (for instance the ED team or the radiology department) to concentrate on these specific aspects of the pathway, rather than expending time and energy on factors out of their control. Those are things which only somebody else can fix.

In this way, the Imaging team, say, can look at their own performance. They can consider the time taken to perform and report a CT scan on a patient from ED and take steps to address any gap between actual performance and the agreed standard.

Breaking down performance by areas such as Majors (seeing sicker patients) and the Urgent Treatment Centre (seeing minor injuries and ailments) allows higher level oversight and coordination of effort. A performance gap in Majors, which is more dependent on specialist team input and bed availability, needs a different set of fixes compared to a gap in UTC, where most patients are seen and discharged by the ED team within the department.

This sort of analysis of performance by area allows the agenda to move away from viewing individual service components in silos, towards a focus on process and teamwork. Such a shift may also be driven by analysis of outcomes. We might compare for instance, performance for patients who are admitted for inpatient care against those who are discharged to home from the ED.

Daily monitoring and assessment of performance includes Breach Analysis, whereby each patient who spends longer than 4 hours in the department has their care pathway analysed. Using an established algorithm, all such breaches are attributed to a cause, such as 'ED long wait', 'Bed delay', 'Imaging delay' and 'Specialty review delay'. Although this enables individual cases to be studied and lessons learnt, it carries a significant downside in attributing individual account-ability (which human nature often translates into blame) in a complex environment with multiple interdependencies.

Perhaps, in the days of a decade ago, when daily breaches of the 4 hour standard would routinely be counted in single figures, such an approach had its merits. In pressured, current-day practice this can all too easily become an exercise in avoiding blame for numerous breaches. It may exacerbate the risk of staff, working hard with limited resource, feeling bullied or harassed in the workplace. The challenge now is for UCLH to reconsider how performance is analysed, in order to feel sure that our data translates into useful information and that our processes enable intelligent healthcare.

There are further benefits of this adaptive, learning cycle approach based on com-paring what we got with what we wanted and correcting accordingly. Embedding measurement requires that the process uses real-time (or very near real-time) data about performance; the cycle time for reporting and error correction must be less than the cycle time for the process. As that information is available locally to the pro-cess itself, it provides corrective and pre-emptive capability for locally empowered citizens. It does not require intervention, permission or decision from other layers in a hierarchy, it does not require extensive reporting and it eradicates the need for post-hoc data mining. Information required by higher order managers in the system can be provided through aggregation with accuracy guaranteed by the design of the system. Performance in such a system is not confined to budgetary control or profitability, but extends to multiple parameters covering whichever aspects of the process are necessary for achieving the intended output and contributing to the desired outcome. In the case of the nation, some of the outcomes belong to indi-viduals, some to the politicians at various levels and, of course, some to the Nation (people) as a whole. What goes well can be celebrated and what doesn't will largely rectify itself within the existing process design. The system is sustainable within a well-defined envelope, with parameters defined by the relationship between the system and its environment and informed by the choices, options and preferences of its human actors. The mechanism of reporting now being understood, attention can turn to those aspects of performance that should be measured, recognising that they are not posed as alternatives but as complementary, interacting to produce a blend of desired outcomes.

Dimensions of performance

Collectively, the citizens of any nation (including its politicians) have to decide what is important to them, but for the purposes of finishing this book, we need to have a list. What is proposed to commence a debate is a list of five dimensions of outcome performance that seems to support the idea of an intelligent nation; it is of the essence of the debate to propose changes and alternatives. Each of the five has two levels of consideration:

> What is the gap between current capability and current performance?
> What is the gap between current performance and future potential?

These questions will be recognised as those embedded in the homeostat and which drive systemic adaptation; continuing improvement at operational and strategic levels. The order of the list has been given some thought but is not definitive as each is of equal importance and the reporting structure will focus attention where it matters; the priorities for attention will reveal themselves:

> Democratic Engagement:
>> Citizens are responsible for and embedded in the processes of their own governance
> Psychological Security:
>> Citizens and the country do not feel threatened or unsafe;
> Economic Security:
>> Citizens and the country are financially prudent and sound;
> Resilience:
>> Citizens and the country are able to sustain activity despite disruptive shocks and restore activity after severe disruption;
> Adaptiveness:
>> Citizens and the country are both responding to and generating changes which ensure a symbiotic relationship with exogenous factors

These five outcomes cannot of course be achieved on their own, they must be underpinned by processes generating outputs that contribute to them. Such processes will need to deal with a range of operational outputs which it seems appropriate to broadly align with both the infrastructure sectors and goals for sustainable development[4]. The infrastructure sectors include:

> Fundamental: Energy, Water, ICT, Transport, Waste
>
> Social: Commerce, Civil Administration, Health, Education, Defence

The United Nations (UN) Development Programme goals help to give an operational dimension and norm for some of those including:

> Ending poverty, hunger, gender inequality (and we should add inequality in relation to sexuality, race and disability);
>
> Promoting good health, well-being and education, sustainable employment, industry and commerce;
>
> Providing infrastructure and access to energy, water and sanitation, digital technology and communication;
>
> Developing liveable communities, towns and cities;
>
> Inhibiting damage to the lived environment on land, water and air and minimising human-driven climate change;
>
> Governance mechanisms and institutions to underpin justice and peace.

The two sets of requirements map together well and the UN goals provide us with a means of comprehending what may be considered important and need measurement. It is important that the specifics of standards and definitions (e.g. definitions of poverty or health and well-being) are for individual countries to decide according to their means and aspirations. There is also a need to recognise that there will be, for many nations and dependent on their natural resources, some degree of reliance on other nations for materials, food, expertise, maybe even water so the strength and resilience of supply chains will be a critical matter. The overarching consideration in all of this will be the establishment of hope and aspiration among the citizens of any particular country and their translation to governmental, corporate and individual actions. If we are to see, as we have with certain countries in the latter part of the 20th and the early part of the 21st centuries, the emergence of strong, independent and resilient nations acting in harmony with others, that will require political leadership. The remaining challenge is to establish a mechanism through which this diverse array of complex dimensions can be brought together and synthesised into a coherent whole.

The potentiometer

If it is not adequate either to report everything on a single figure or to take two or three notionally independent figures and offset rather than integrate them, then we must develop a mechanism which both places measurement of performance in a common format and synthesises the results in an aggregating framework enabling the meaningful comparison of very different things. The complex set of output measures identified will not lend themselves to a conventionally homogeneous set of representations, which would risk exposing the whole to a charge of attempting to compare or compound things vastly different and non-comparable. The answers to the questions 'how safe am I' and 'how rich am I' demand very different approaches, yet the same device needs to represent them.

The mechanism for resolving the challenge is what Beer (1981) called the 'potentiometer' (Figure 6.2), a device that, for any particular moment and configuration tells us 'THIS is what you said you were capable of doing, THAT is what you did, HERE is the difference'. It represents results not as an absolute number but as a ratio showing what proportion of capability was actually achieved. Beckford (2020) provides insights additional to those that now follow. Using ratios, the potentiometer enables comparison between things which are heterogeneous; which is a core requirement if we are to bring together the multiple dimensions of our performance envelope. It will allow us to compare apples with pears.

Having determined that results will be most usefully expressed as ratios to enable performance comparison, the starting point for the potentiometer is to understand the CAPABILITY of the system under consideration. Without leaping (yet) to the very specific, capability is an operational definition of the capacities of the process to be considered. The capability in any given time period is underpinned with the calculation of an available output, volume or frequency. For any process, an 'output per time period' would be a function of the combination and interactions of inputs such as materials, data, skills, money. For transparency and to enable adaptation, the underpinning calculations that amount to capability along with the assumptions and specifications must be available as they are dynamic.

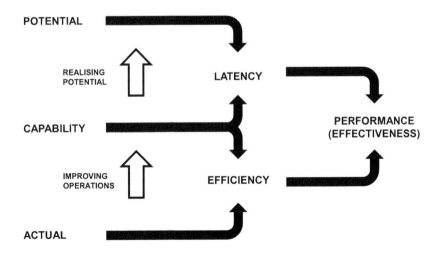

FIGURE 6.2 The potentiometer

What capability means in practice is a function of the underlying sum from which it is derived.

The ACTUAL figure is derived from precisely the same sum as the CAPABILITY except the number inserted in the potentiometer is the output actually achieved, hence ACTUAL, rather than that which was targeted or believed achievable. The proportion between the two is stated as an efficiency or productivity ratio:

> the amount of output that could have been achieved divided by the amount of output that was achieved = EFFICIENCY

Improving operations means, in the most conventional sense, improving actual output to the level of capability. This is achieved by increasing yield, reducing waste, some combination thereof or modifying the statement of capability, if the level set is found under actual constraints to be unachievable. It could mean, for example, reducing the materials or energy used, applying skills or data more appropriately, applying behaviours differently. If the appropriate skills are not available, then perhaps capability needs to be reduced. Where a process relies on people more than it does machines, the skills and behaviour dimension of process performance become critical. The responsibility and therefore the autonomy to apply improvement necessarily belong to the people who operate the process under consideration and their freedom to do so should be constrained only by adherence to the agreed product or service. That is, they must do what they can to improve the product or service within the constraints that exist. They do not have the freedom to either change the product or service or to change higher order constraints (although they can alert managers to their existence). The potentiometer at this point is accurately indicating the efficiency of the particular process at a given point in time or perhaps over an accumulated number of process cycles (a time series of events). Improvement in the ratio (increase in efficiency as measured) over time helps us understand levels of improvement.

Realising POTENTIAL means overcoming the constraints that currently limit CAPABILITY, whatever they may be, so that the hopes and aspirations can be attained. Here again the concern is with understanding a ratio, in this case of the amount of output that could be achieved if constraints were removed, divided by the amount of output that can be achieved by the current process = LATENCY.

Here the aim is to remove or overcome constraints on the process thereby getting closer to the scale of the potential (the ambition or opportunity). Again, there is a learning loop in which review of the drivers of latency is the mechanism for adapting the system. At this stage, the potentiometer is revealed as the informational equivalent of the control devices in the homeostat, embedding both measurement and adaptation in the process itself.

The overall aim is to understand the extent to which the process fulfils its purpose, that is, achieves the outcome for which it was established. The calculation for this is to multiply the efficiency by the latency; this defines the overall scope for improvement or the extent to which purpose remains unfulfilled; it defines

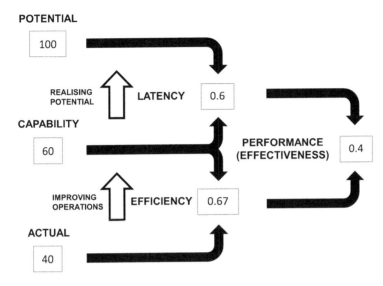

FIGURE 6.3 The potentiometer with ratios

the effectiveness of the system. If we look at Figure 6.3, the ratio boxes have been populated.

Presented for illustrative purposes, Figure 6.3 shows us that

A process has a current CAPABILITY of 60 units of output;
In the time period, it has an ACTUAL output of 40 units:
The EFFICIENCY ratio is 40/60 = 0.67, that is, the actual output could be increased by 20 units (0.33) within the current constraints.

CAPABILITY is currently constrained and it is understood that, with constraints lifted, the process has a POTENTIAL of 100 units.
The LATENCY ratio is 60/100 = 0.6, that is, if the current constraints were lifted, the capability could be increased by 40 units (0.4).

The measure of EFFECTIVENESS of the process is a function of its EFFICIENCY multiplied by its LATENCY (or its ACTUAL divided by its POTENTIAL – the product is the same) which is: 0.6*0.67 = 0.4.

EFFECTIVENESS is 0.4; the process has the potential to produce an additional 60 units of output.

What can now be appreciated is that in stating the potential of any system in the potentiometer, that potential is an expression of purpose, the measure of success. Effectiveness is a statement of the extent to which purpose has been fulfilled.

The fulfilment of output and outcome in any organisation is rarely a product of a single process and, to apply improvement effort where it can deliver the greatest gain, the points of engagement where meaningful difference can be made need to be identified. Figure 6.4 shows a process potentiometer, one which uses the results from each stage in a process to inform the next. This particular case is deliberately linear at this point, chosen for the purposes of explanation. The example is that of a paper mill, recycling fibre to produce paper for the newspaper trade and is only concerned with production not sales. The production process is Recycle, Process, Make (on one of two machines of different capacities) and Wind (again on one of two machines of different capacities). Capability is calculated in this case by understanding the specification of the machines, the utilisation of the machines and the budget of the mill (in effect a constraint on performance). The calculations are all laid out in Figure 6.5, the process performance dashboard. Critically where two stages are interdependent (Recycle and Process), the performance of the first constrains the performance of the second and so on, you can see in the figure that the 'actual' output of 'Recycle' becomes the 'capability' of 'Process'. If we want more performance from the Process element, we must first get it from the Recycle element.

Looking at Figure 6.4, we can see that while the process efficiency of the second stage is 0.96 (i.e. it achieves 96% of capability), it only achieves 71% of its potential because its capability is constrained by the output of the previous activity, which you can see is only achieving 80% efficiency. These constraints then flow through the entire process. If more throughput is to be achieved, that can only be done by improving the first activity and then chasing the improvement through the mill. This demonstrates the importance of dealing with the system as a whole not just the parts. When this model was applied in the real situation, a substantial step increase in output was delivered in a very short time period. The process potentiometer is not simply revealing what the situation is, it is also indicating why it is like that and where to apply improvement effort and all as a consequence of simply making the paper. No additional work is required; performance control (error correcting feedback) adaptiveness at two levels has been designed into the organisation.

The process performance dashboard (Figure 6.5) serves three functions. First, it tells the operator about the specification setting of each machine, showing how well they are utilising the process and showing the scope for improving efficiency and effectiveness. Second, it shows how the numbers in the specification translate into output performance for each stage and for the whole mill. Third, it allows the operators to simulate the effects of changes in the settings of each machine and allows them to optimise performance in real time.

The dashboard generates the potential for both feedback and feedforward control by allowing the result of changes in the settings and specifications to be examined and hence enabling the management to create the future for the organisation; an additional characteristic of adaptive organisation. The feedback loops are included in Figure 6.6 and shows how information flows bidirectionally through the process enabling self-regulation and operational adaptation in near real time.

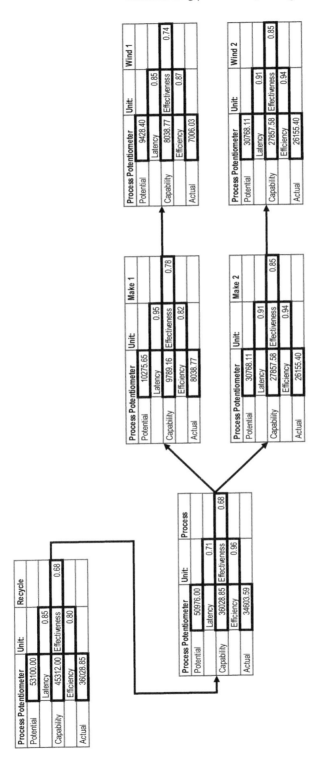

FIGURE 6.4 Process potentiometer

Input / Target / Output analysis

	Input 39656.00 Potential	Capability (Unit)	Capability (Process)	Target 40000 Most Likely	Output 36664.22 Latency (Unit)	Latency (Process)	Productivity (Unit)	Productivity (Process)	Performance (Unit)	Performance (Process)	Back	Possible	Translation
Recycle	53100.00	39656.00	39656.00	36028.85	0.75	0.75	0.91	1.00	0.75	0.68	40000.00	39656.00	1
Process	50976.00	49080.00	39656.00	34603.59	0.96	0.96	0.87	0.81	0.78	0.84	40000.00	39656.00	1
Make 1 & 2	41043.76	36664.22	36664.22	35242.67	0.89	0.89	0.96	1.00	0.89	0.86	42920.00	49080.00	1.073
Wind 1 & 2	60743.38	55852.16	36664.22	36166.08	0.92	0.92	0.99	0.66	0.60	0.91	40000.00	36664.22	1

Recycle — Settings

	Unit	Process
Limit	37.50	36.00
Rate	32.00	33.00
Lines	2.00	2.00
Hours	20.00	24.00
Days	31.00	31.00
Pshut	12.00	12.00
UpShut	12.00	12.00
Target	39656.00	49080.00

Make — Settings

	Make 1	Make 2
Limit	910.00	1700.00
Rate	905.00	1650.00
Width	5.40	9.40
Weight	48.50	48.50
Lines	1.00	1.00
Hours	24.00	44.60
Days	31.00	31.00
Pshuts	2.80%	2.90%
UpShuts	5.80%	3.00%
Breaks	3.00%	0.90%
JR Loss	0.90%	0.90%
Beater	3.00%	3.00%
Gross	10580.55	30879.54
Net	8940.57	27723.65
Unit max	10275.65	30768.11
Sum 1&2		36664.22

Wind / Rewind — Settings

	Wind 1	Wind 2	Rewind	Settings
Limit	1700.00	1000.00	1200.00	1000.00
Weight	1650.00	48.50	44.60	44.60
Width	9.40	5.40	9.40	9.40
Hours	44.60	20.00	20.00	20.00
Tloss	1.00	3.50%	2.48%	0.00%
JR Loss	24.00	0.90%	0.90%	0.00%
Beater	31.00	3.00%	0.52%	0.00%
Cull	2.90%	1.00%	1.00%	0.00%
Pshuts	2.90%	2.80%	2.90%	0.00%
UpShuts	3.00%	5.80%	2.90%	0.00%
Breaks	0.90%	3.00%	3.00%	0.00%
Lines	0.52%	1.00	2.00	1.00
No. of Days	31.00	31.00	31.00	31.00
Gross	30879.54	9401.69	36501.49	15595.73
Net	27723.65	7850.41	32406.02	15595.73
Unit Max	30768.11	9428.40	36222.34	15092.64
Sum 1&2	36664.22		55852.16	55852.16

FIGURE 6.5 Process performance dashboard

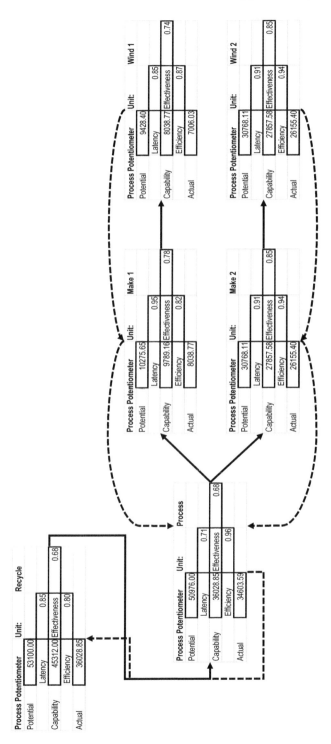

FIGURE 6.6 Process potentiometer with feedback

A country is more complicated than a single paper mill but the principle of using such tools is not. Once it is understood how the country is organised, this approach can be applied to all of its processes at different levels of consideration. Across all areas of policy, such an approach in combination with the earlier call to be explicit about desired outcomes, would demand that politicians be clear about ambition, clear about the extent to which that ambition is met (or not), stimulate increased visible accountability and increase citizen engagement in decision-making.

The compound potentiometer

In order to manage the Intelligent Nation as an explicitly adaptive system, an over-all performance-reporting information architecture that enables and drives that ambition must be crafted. Performance management must be embedded first in the trialogue and then in the overall supporting organisational framework, the struc-tural model of an Intelligent Nation which was explored in Chapter 2. The organ-isational framework allows the continuous re-optimisation of central and local control. That structure needs to accommodate the individual, community, regional and national perspectives which are recursively embedded inside each other and developed here as Figure 6.7, as well as the more functional arrangements of the

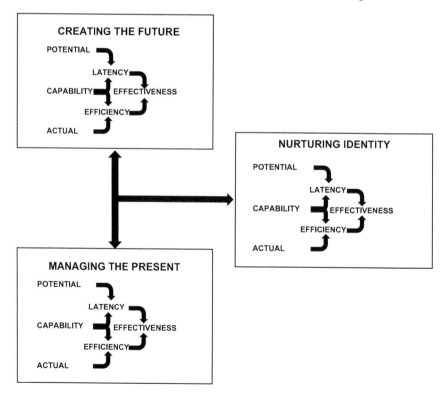

FIGURE 6.7 Trialogue potentiometers

multiple infrastructure sectors. That means compiling performance measurement in two dimensions: horizontal (across sectors) and vertical (through the organisational hierarchy). Doing so will reveal how each element is performing locally, what actions can be taken at that level to improve it and what is in the gift of higher authority:

- what can I do in my house;
- what can WE do in our local community;
- what can THEY do at regional level;
- what MUST be done by central government only.

This approach will be most effective and fastest when the autonomy of the smallest parts is maximised within the constraints of belongingness. The more information needs to be channelled up and down the necessary hierarchy, the slower will be the pace, the more remote the control, the less efficient the whole. Embedding potentiometers in the trialogue (Figure 6.7) will enable and inform managerial action, embedding information for self-regulation in the management process through which the organisation seeks to do things better (managing the present), do better things (creating the future) and define better (nurturing identity).

Within each of those elements, there is a double loop of continuous improvement, closing the gaps between actual and capability and between capability and potential, while synthesising the desired outcome (the pursuit of purpose) by continually resolving the tension between the demands of the present and the desires of the future – an authentic conversation demanding prudence and probity.

Figure 6.8 shows how those trialogues are embedded in the organisational architecture. Through the evaluations at each level (self, local government, regional government, national government), they generate conversations, a dialogue, about performance between the different organisational levels. The electoral process acts as a regulator of the conversation, granting it democratic legitimacy but with a dependence on the periodicity of elections.

The activity of 'Regulation' is currently carried out in the UK by organisations such as ORR and Ofgem, in the USA by FERC (for energy) while in France, no single agency is currently responsible for water regulation though the Water Agencies are supervised by the Ministry of Ecology AND the Ministry of Economy and Finance. In the model of the Intelligent Nation, the role of the regulator will need to be responsive to the business and ownership models and regulation will need to be applied, not principally to the economic performance but to a wider range of matters linked to the desired national outcomes. In Figures 6.8 and 6.9, these regulators are best considered as embedded in the elements of the trialogues rather than as separate functions. To avoid further over-centralisation, regulation is distributed at the different levels so that the bulk of regulation occurs at the 'local authority' level, with higher order interventions only where necessary to enable alignment with national objectives. A good

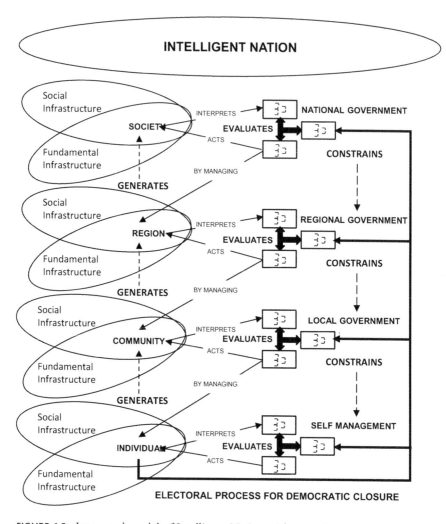

FIGURE 6.8 Integrated model of Intelligent Nation with potentiometers

example of this would be the regulation of resilience. A local regulator may be responsible for the overall performance of the utilities in their locality, aiming to optimise local performance, while the regulator at the regional level could be responsible for ensuring utilities are resilient across the boundaries, perhaps even funding that element of provision as part of a national policy. Efficiency would then be pursued locally while effectiveness is pursued at the regional or national levels.

Figure 6.9 can be thought of as an orthogonal slice through Figure 6.7, presenting a functional perspective on the interactions, delineated by the stars, between the elements of fundamental and social infrastructure. Based on the notion of society emerging (drawn from Figure 3.2), it shows how the performance of each element

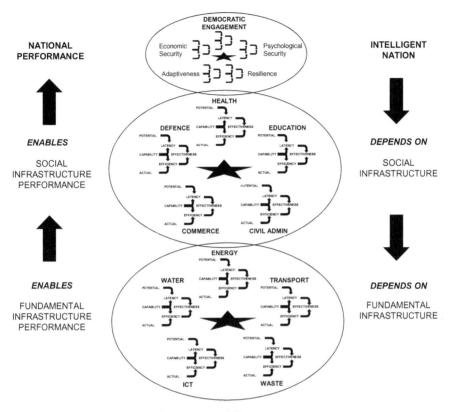

FIGURE 6.9   Infrastructure performance modelling

is interdependent with the others, the collective results acting first as the enabler of social infrastructure, then to society. Society in this case may refer to the 'self-managed' individual, the local, regional or national governmental levels. The results of this process do not compile or aggregate into a single figure but, as represented in Figure 6.10, provide a dashboard showing all the dimensions at two levels, efficiency and latency, and the performance of each relative to the others. The dashboard not only provides information about the current state of affairs but also indicates where the biggest gains can be achieved.

Governance and the Intelligent Nation

At the beginning of this chapter, it was suggested that the use of GDP as a measure of national performance was wholly inadequate to the task even setting aside the lack of agreement about its meaning, structure and utility.

Through the chapter, a model of performance management has been proposed which is much richer than GDP. Rather than offering a series of different ways of thinking and measuring, the model seeks to integrate the coherent set of

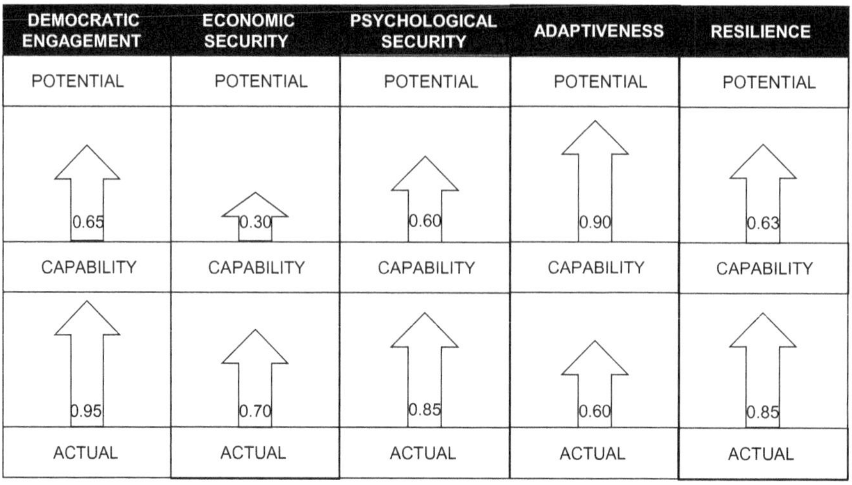

DEMOCRATIC ENGAGEMENT	ECONOMIC SECURITY	PSYCHOLOGICAL SECURITY	ADAPTIVENESS	RESILIENCE
POTENTIAL	POTENTIAL	POTENTIAL	POTENTIAL	POTENTIAL
0.65	0.30	0.60	0.90	0.63
CAPABILITY	CAPABILITY	CAPABILITY	CAPABILITY	CAPABILITY
0.95	0.70	0.85	0.60	0.85
ACTUAL	ACTUAL	ACTUAL	ACTUAL	ACTUAL

FIGURE 6.10   National performance dashboard

dimensions any country might seek to measure into the coherent national framework of the Intelligent Nation. This uses a consistent mechanism of performance reporting embedded in the structure of the decision-making. This is no more easy to develop, describe and write than it is to understand – and it will certainly take more than one reading. Persist.

The Intelligent Nation, in fact any nation, is a complex, dynamic, interacting and interdependent mess of people, organisations, systems, processes, behaviours, politics, preferences and biases. All those things must be accommodated in the ways they are managed. Of course, what is offered here is not perfect; its task is to make all think more deeply, to reflect on what is important to them and to raise their democratic voice in its pursuit.

This book started with an assertion about the inadequacy of existing and historic structures and bureaucratic arrangements of the government, the state and democratic legitimacy. An alternative has been offered, consciously naïve in places, intended as a starting point for a radical transformation. Now is the time for action, for politicians, public servants of all types and grades and citizens, for whose benefit all of this is intended, to get to grips with the problem. A friend of mine, working in a large public service facility, said to me one day: 'John, we all know that about 30% of our time, energy and resources are wasted'. I tested that with a number of other people in other organisations, most argued with the proportion, none argued with the principle. So, if that is roughly true then think about this – we can EITHER spend around 30% less on public services OR have 30% more public services (or some blend of the two) – what might the impact of that be? Our arguments should not be about more resources, postcode lotteries or selective deprivation, but about what outcomes we value and how more of them can be realised by the adoption of the ideas of the Intelligent Nation.

Key points

-   Traditional means of reporting are inadequate for an Intelligent Nation which is thought of as a complex adaptive system;
-   Measurement of GDP is unhelpful as a basis of managing a modern nation; it has no agreed meaning and places emphasis on only one aspect;
-   Systemic interdependence has been established between the productive and non-productive elements of the country;
-   Triple bottom line and other multi-measure approaches remain inadequate because they seek to pose different achievements as alternative not complementary;
-   Governance is integral to an Intelligent Nation; it requires that management is built in to processes not added on; it requires the engagement of people in the process of governing;
-   Any alternative system of reporting must embrace multiple characteristics in an envelope of complementary dimensions based on 'and' not 'or';
-   Sustainability is joint, several, interdependent and co-evolutionary;
-   A dynamic system experiences uncertainty in all aspects of measurement; space must be maintained for judgement to be exercised and its successes and failures learned from;
-   Cybernetics offers tools, the homeostat and the potentiometer to assist with integrating performance reporting with processes;
-   Dimensions of performance need to be debated and agreed, then reported through a mechanism that allows the management of multiple dimensions of performance simultaneously.

References

Beckford, J., (2020) *The Intelligent Organisation: Driving Systemic Change with Information*, 2nd edition, Routledge, London

Beer, S., (1981) *Brain of the Firm*, Wiley, Chichester

Beinhocker, E., (2007) *The Origin of Wealth: Evolution, Complexity, and the Radical Remaking of Economics*, Random House, London

Braithwaite, J., (2008) *Regulatory Capitalism*, Edward Elgar Publishing, Cheltenham, UK

Henriques, A. and Richardson, J. (eds), (2004) *The Triple Bottom Line*, Earthscan, London

Huff, D., (1991) *How to Lie with Statistics*, Penguin, London

Lovelock, J., (1995) *Gaia: A New Look at Life on Earth*, Oxford University Press, Oxford

Mazzucato, M., (2018) *The Value of Everything*, Penguin, London

Meadows, D., et al. (1972) *The Limits to Growth*, Potomac Associates, Universe Books, New York

Muller, J.Z., (2018) *The Tyranny of Metrics*, Princeton University Press, Oxford

OECD, (1975) *The Polluter Pays Principle*, OECD, Paris

Raworth, K., (2018) *Doughnut Economics*, Random House Business, London

Taguchi, G., (1987) *Systems of Experimental Design*, Vols 1 and 2, Unipub/Kraus International Publications, New York

Waddington, C.H., (1977) *Tools for Thought*, Cape, London

Notes

1. https://medium.com/iipp-blog/capitalism-done-right-a-co-operative-system-to-solvehuman-problems-25d2ca91e9a5 30/04/2020
2. https://www.londonsociety.org.uk/post/whenthisisallover-lord-toby-harris 01/05/2020
3. https://beckfordconsulting.com/misc/covid-19-the-necessity-of-evolving-wisdom/ 01/05/2020
4. https://www.undp.org/content/undp/en/home/sustainable-development-goals.html

Index

Page numbers in *italic* indicate figures and page numbers in **bold** indicate tables.